SCHOLASTIC

ACTIVE™ Grammar

Practice Book 6

Rosemary Allen

Name ____

Class ____

Previously published as Grammar Skills 6 by Learners Publishing Pte Ltd.

First edition 2012
Reprinted 2012, 2013, 2014 (thrice), 2015 (fourth time), 2016, 2017, 2018, 2019 (twice), 2020, 2021, 2022, 2023, 2024, 2025

ISBN 978-81-8477-751-2

CONTENTS

 ISBN 978-81-8477-751-2

To Teachers and Parents

The study of English grammar in schools is changing as educators become increasingly aware of the important role context plays in language learning. The functional use of grammar has become a feature of English syllabuses around the world.

Active Grammar Practice Books have been written specifically to provide students with valuable links between basic, traditional grammatical concepts and the functional contexts in which they are used. The activities represent a blend of traditional and functional approaches to describe how texts 'work' in real-life situations and why certain grammatical choices are considered appropriate. Traditional grammar serves to provide students with the special terminology needed to talk about grammar, while functional grammar is intended to improve communicative competence by showing students how grammar works in the context of different text types.

The exercises in this book give students systematic guidance in developing an understanding of grammatical concepts. Throughout the books there are panel notes that give hints for correct usage and highlight exceptions to grammar rules, as well as provide simple non-technical definitions to help students understand the exercises. Many of the exercises incorporate learner-centred activities that include completing rhymes and short stories, solving riddles and puzzles, doing word searches and seeing 'language-in-action'. At the same time, the activities provide teachers with a range of techniques to use, techniques that have proven highly successful with both native and non-native speakers of English. The exercises are graded, but include challenging ones to motivate as well as interest the students.

It is hoped that teachers will find this series a valuable tool in their teaching programme, one that will provide young learners with a fascinating journey into the world of English language and a sound knowledge of how it works.

 ISBN 978-81-8477-751-2

1 Articles and Nouns

Grammar Help

The **indefinite articles** are **a** and **an**.

- Use **a** before a noun that starts with a consonant sound (boy, university).
- Use **an** before a noun that starts with a vowel sound.
- Use **an** before a noun that has a silent "h" (hour).

A *Who is speaking? The words in the box will help you. Remember to use* **a** *or* **an** *in your answer. The first is done for you.*

acrobat	**announcer**	**architect**	**auctioneer**
caddie	**chauffeur**	**heiress**	**herald**
judge	**milliner**	**ornithologist**	

1. I introduce radio and television programmes. I'm an announcer.
2. I perform tricks and do handsprings. ______
3. I carry a golfer's clubs when he plays. ______
4. I am employed to drive a car. ______
5. I design buildings. ______
6. I make and sell ladies' hats. ______
7. I inherited a lot of money. ______
8. I sell goods to the highest bidder. ______
9. I preside over a law court. ______
10. I study birds. ______
11. I am an official messenger. ______

 ISBN 978-81-8477-751-2

Grammar Help

Use the indefinite articles **a** and **an** when you mention something for the first time. When you refer to it again, use the definite article **the**. The definite article is also used when you are referring to a particular one, such as ***the*** *Singapore River.*

B ***Complete the sentences by adding definite or indefinite articles.***

Perth is (1) ________ very beautiful city. Situated on (2) ________ Swan River, it is (3) ________ capital city of (4) ________ state of Western Australia. Visitors to Perth always visit King's Park, which is (5) ________ scenic, natural bush area overlooking (6) ________ city. In the park, there is (7) ________ war memorial from which visitors can see (8) ________ whole city, as well as (9) ________ tributaries of (10) ________ Swan River. In the park, there is also (11) ________ cross-section of (12) ________ ancient tree that gives (13) ________ insight into how old some of the Western Australian trees are. You will certainly want to see (14) ________ wildflowers. (15) ________ wildflower festival is held in spring every year.

Grammar Help

- The definite article **the** can be used with both singular and plural nouns.
- The definite article is not used when a place is visited or used for its normal purpose, but is used when you are referring to a particular one. For example: *We went to church on Sunday.* ***The*** *church I go to is on the hill.*

C ***Complete the sentences by adding an article when necessary. Leave the space blank if an article is not needed.***

Christopher Columbus, (1) ________ famous explorer, was born in (2) ________ Genoa in Italy in 1451, but left (3) ________ home to live in Spain.

 ISBN 978-81-8477-751-2

On 3 August 1492, Columbus set out to (4) __________ sea with (5) __________ crew of 90 men and three ships. Before setting (6) __________ sail, he went to (7) __________ church to pray for (8) __________ uneventful and safe journey. He knew (9) __________ crew was anxious to go to (10) __________ sea, although many believed (11) __________ Earth was flat and feared (12) __________ ship would fall off (13) __________ edge of (14) __________ world if they went too far west.

During (15) __________ voyage, they passed many whales. In those days, (16) __________ whale was not in danger of extinction and (17) __________ sailors feared (18) __________ huge mammal because (19) __________ collision with one of them could cause damage to (20) __________ ship. They also saw (21) __________ sailfish leaping from (22) __________ water and caught many strange fish.

On (23) __________ morning of 12 October, (24) __________ sailor on board (25) __________ *Pinta*, let out (26) __________ excited yell. He had sighted (27) __________ large island. At (28) __________ daylight, Columbus and (29) __________ crew went ashore and planted (30) __________ flag of Spain in (31) __________ sand. Instead of finding (32) __________ new route to (33) __________ Far East, Columbus's ships had landed in (34) __________ Bahamas.

 ISBN 978-81-8477-751-2

Grammar Help

Some adjectives behave like nouns when you place **the** in front of them; for example, *the* ***rich****, the* ***aged***. It is like a short way for saying "the rich people".

D ***In the box below are some adjectives that behave like nouns. Use them to fill in the blanks in the article.***

the educated	**the adventurous**	**the rich**	**the poor**
the generous	**the less fortunate**	**the aged**	**the sick**

There are many ways we can help (1) the less fortunate in our society. Some of (2) ____________ and (3) ____________ need transport to their doctors, as they are too ill or too old to travel on their own. Many poorer students experience difficulty with their schoolwork and need help from (4) ____________. Extra money for basic food items is also needed by (5) ____________. Charitable organizations play an important role in reaching out to (6) ____________ and (7) ____________ to provide donations of money. The Singapore International Foundation is for (8) ____________ who want to help in overseas projects.

 ISBN 978-81-8477-751-2

2 Quantifiers

Grammar Help

Quantifiers are words used to tell about number or amount when the exact amount is not known or not specific. Examples are: ***some, few, any, every, many, most, each, several, a little, more, plenty*** and ***no.***

- The quantifiers **much**, **little** and **less** are used with uncountable nouns.
- The quantifiers **many**, **few** and **fewer** are used with plural countable nouns.

A ***Imagine you live in an isolated place. Your food supplies are running very low. You are recording the provisions you have left. Choose the correct quantifiers to complete the sentences in your record below.***

1. We have ______________ (a few, a little) oranges and apples.
2. We have ______________(any, some) cheese, but we do not have ______________ (plenty, much) jam or bread left.
3. We also have ______________ (any, some) carrots and potatoes.
4. There's only ______________ (some, a little) sugar and tea left; not much.
5. We don't have ______________ (some, much) water either.
6. I think we have ______________ (much, more) milk than orange juice.
7. We don't have ______________ (some, any) chocolate bars left.
8. We ate ______________ (all, many) of the chocolate bars yesterday.
9. Fortunately, we still have ______________ (many, some) biscuits.
10. We have ______________(several, much) packets of instant noodles and ______________ (plenty, much) of instant soup too.

 ISBN 978-81-8477-751-2

Grammar Help

To talk about things singly, or individually, you use **each**, but to talk about things together, or as a group, you use **every** or **all**, for example: ***Each*** *child prepared a different act for the concert.* ***Every*** *child performed in the concert.*

- A plural verb is used with **all**, for example: ***All*** *roads* ***are*** *under repair.*
- A singular verb is used with **each** and **every**, for example: ***Every/Each*** *road* ***is*** *under repair.*
- You can use **all**, but not **every**, with uncountable nouns, for example: *Jane likes* ***all*** *music.*

B ***Choose the correct quantifier to fill in each blank in these sentences about preparing for an art exhibition.***

1. Come on, everyone, we don't have ________________ time.
(a) much (b) little (c) many (d) few

2. Let ________________ of us try to help each other.
(a) every (b) another (c) all (d) any

3. There are very ________________ students who are willing to help.
(a) few (b) little (c) a few (d) plenty

4. We have ________________ work to do before the art room is ready.
(a) a lot of (b) any (c) all (d) many

5. There are ________________ art pieces to display than we had last year.
(a) many (b) more (c) most (d) few

6. I expect ________________ students to do their best to make this art show a success.
(a) any (b) every (c) plenty of (d) all

7. In the past, students have shown ________________ interest in exhibiting their work.
(a) little (b) any (c) many (d) several

8. This year, the students have been ________________ enthusiastic.
(a) plenty (b) much (c) few (d) most

 ISBN 978-81-8477-751-2

9. Now we have very little space to hang __________ the art pieces.
(a) a lot of (b) all (c) a few (d) every

10. I hope we have __________ visitors to the art show this time.
(a) few (b) much (c) little (d) many

Grammar Help

- **Either** and **neither** are usually used with singular verbs. You use **either** when you speak about "one or the other". You use **neither** when you mean "not one nor the other".
- To talk about two things together, you use **both**, for example: ***Both*** *the cat and the dog belong to James.* You use a plural verb with **both**.
- You usually use **another** with singular countable nouns, for example: *Shall I pass you* ***another*** *slice of cake?*
- **Another** is also used before the word **few** or with numbers, for example: *Give me* ***another few*** *minutes. Give me* ***another three*** *minutes.*

C *Complete the following dialogue using* **both, either, neither** *or* **another**.

Mother: Jane, I asked you to clean your bedroom and bathe the dog. You have done (1) __________ task. Now you have time to do only one of them; so which will it be?

Jane: Sorry, Mum, I don't mind (2) __________ one. I was doing my homework. Please give me (3) __________ few minutes and I'll try to do (4) __________ tasks.

Mother: You should have told me you were busy. (5) __________ James or John could have bathed the dog. (6) __________ has any homework today.

Jane: If (7) __________ one of them can do it for me today, I'll do the same for him (8) __________ day when he has lots of homework.

Mother: I'll call (9) __________ of them in to see who will volunteer. You can clean your room (10) __________ day instead.

 ISBN 978-81-8477-751-2

D ***Read the passage below and circle eight quantifiers. Then underline the verbs and write "S" above the verb if it is used in the singular and write "P" above it if it is used in the plural. The first one has been done for you.***

Sometimes it seems as if every road in my area is (S) under repair. Each day brings with it a new detour. In fact, both roads leading to my house are currently having traffic lights installed and I have been told that another few roads close by are to be resurfaced too. It seems that every person in the area has been inconvenienced. However, both guards at the bank in the locality say that all traffic lights are going to be operational in a day or two. I'm happy to say that all traffic is now to be diverted back to the main road.

 ISBN 978-81-8477-751-2

Grammar Help

Uncountable nouns are not used with the indefinite article, ***a*** or ***an***. They may be preceded by quantifiers such as ***some, any, no*** or ***a little***. Quantifiers may consist of more than one word, as in: *Please pass me* ***a glass of*** *water.*

E ***Complete the recount below, using suitable quantifiers from the box.***

a packet of	a cup of	a cake of	some
a few drops of	a block of	a little	no
a few grains of	a piece of	a slice of	much
a bag of	a pane of		

My mother had a disastrous day yesterday. While taking a shower, she slipped on (1) ________________ soap, which caused her shampoo bottle to fly out of her hand. It hit the window and cracked (2) ________________ glass. She applied (3) ________________ ointment on her injured leg and limped painfully downstairs for breakfast.

The other members of the family had already eaten, and all that was left comprised (4) ________________ jam and (5) ________________ bread. There was (6) ________________ cereal or butter, although there were (7) ________________ juice in the carton and about (8) ________________ milk and (9) ________________ sugar at the bottom of the sugar bowl.

Feeling very hungry, my mother dressed to go shopping, but then remembered she did not have (10) ________________ money — just a few dollars. However, this was enough to buy a few items she needed for the morning. So she took (11) ________________ paper and wrote a shopping list. "I can buy (12) ________________ biscuits for morning tea, (13) ________________ sugar and (14) ________________ butter," she thought. "I will do more shopping this evening with the family. We can have dinner at a restaurant afterwards."

 ISBN 978-81-8477-751-2

3 Nouns: Abstract and Possessive

Grammar Help

Most nouns name things you can see and touch, but **abstract nouns** describe things that can only be thought about. You cannot see or touch them.

You can form abstract nouns by adding suffixes, such as: ***-ability, -acy, -age, -ance, -ence, -ism, -ity, -ment, -ness, -ship*** and ***-tion,*** to some adjectives, verbs or other nouns.

A ***Find 12 abstract nouns in the following passage and underline them. Note that not all the abstract nouns end with a suffix.***

It takes courage to climb a mountain but the young man had plenty of that, as well as boundless enthusiasm and a strong will to succeed.

Although he had been raised in poverty and without a father, he had experienced much happiness and expert guidance from his mother. Thanks to his mother, who viewed education and knowledge as far more important than wealth, he was growing into a person of discipline and dedication.

Both of these qualities would be needed if he were to tackle the dangerous slopes of the towering mountain that had claimed the life of his father.

 ISBN 978-81-8477-751-2

B ***Fill in each blank with a suitable abstract noun. Use the word in brackets to help you.***

1. Something that caged animals long for is ________________ (free).
2. People who share their time and money show ________________ (kind) or ________________ (generous) towards their fellow human beings.
3. Some people who do not make friends easily suffer from ________________ (lonely) even when they are among other people.
4. When people steal, they can be arrested for ________________ (thief).
5. When you are young, that time of your life is your ________________ (child).
6. People who try to make careful and sensible decisions have what is called ________________ (prudent).
7. Tom was rude and disrespectful to his grandmother; so his parents punished him for his ________________ (insolent).
8. People who are forgiving and less strict show ________________ (lenient).
9. Jane did her work carelessly; so she was reprimanded for ________________ (lazy).
10. At home or at school, ________________ (honest) is the best policy.
11. He was green with ________________ (envious) when one of his colleagues was promoted to Sales Manager.
12. They say that ________________ (beautiful) is in the eye of the beholder, but Liza charms everyone she meets.
13. When John was demoted for being arrogant to his boss, a colleague of his said, "________________ (proud) goes before a fall."
14. ________________ (Curious) may kill the cat, but we need it to gain knowledge about the world around us.
15. ________________ (Ignorant) of the law is no excuse for breaking it.

 ISBN 978-81-8477-751-2

C *Can you find 20 abstract nouns in the word puzzle?*

1. Draw a line through each word you find. (The words in the box are the adjective forms.) The nouns could be written across or down.

ambitious	**peaceful**	**beautiful**	**caring**	**brave**
courageous	**energetic**	**fearful**	**forgetful**	**free**
knowledgeable	**honest**	**just**	**modest**	**long**
charitable	**skilled**	**truthful**	**united**	**witty**

C	R	E	A	M	B	I	T	I	O	N	T	H
A	P	E	A	C	E	B	W	I	S	E	W	O
R	E	A	C	H	A	R	I	T	Y	B	A	N
E	L	B	A	J	U	S	T	I	C	E	R	E
F	O	R	G	E	T	F	U	L	N	E	S	S
R	P	A	S	T	Y	E	N	T	A	S	K	T
E	E	V	F	A	T	A	I	J	R	K	T	Y
E	N	E	R	G	Y	R	T	U	G	I	T	O
D	A	R	C	O	W	A	Y	D	U	L	R	W
O	B	Y	C	O	U	R	A	G	E	L	U	E
M	O	D	E	S	T	Y	L	E	N	G	T	H
S	K	N	O	W	L	E	D	G	E	U	H	E

2. Choose six of the words you found in the puzzle and use them in sentences of your own.

(a) ____________________

(b) ____________________

(c) ____________________

(d) ____________________

(e) ____________________

(f) ____________________

 ISBN 978-81-8477-751-2

Grammar Help

Possessive nouns have an apostrophe (') to show that someone owns something. The apostrophe is placed after the owner and an **s** is added if it is necessary.

- If two or more people possess the same thing, the apostrophe followed by **s** is added only to the last noun. For example: *This is Sue and Sally'**s** dog.*
- If the two people own things separately, the nouns for them each have an apostrophe **s** (**'s**). For example: *Joe'**s** collie and Jack'**s** cocker spaniel won awards at the dog show.*
- For compound nouns, only the last word has the apostrophe **s**. For example: *My sister-in-law'**s** brothers are about my age.*

D ***Rewrite each of the following sentences, changing the words in bold to the possessive form.***

1. Jack, **the brother of Richard and John**, is visiting us tomorrow.

____

2. Many **houses of the residents** were destroyed by the strong tornado winds.

____

____

3. **The car belonging to the father of Sarah** was stolen last Friday.

____

4. The **thorns of the rose plant** make the flowers difficult to pick.

____

____

5. The **maids of the princesses** were competitive and always suspicious of the intentions of one another.

____

____

 ISBN 978-81-8477-751-2

6. **The mothers of Peter and Mary** wept at their wedding.

7. **The habit of the hermit crab** of changing its shell as it grows puts it in danger.

8. The volcano erupted and spewed its lava on the town, burning **the homes of many people** and destroying the **main buildings of the town** as well.

9. Jane cleans her own bedroom, but her mother cleans **the bedrooms of her brothers.**

10. **The spokesman for the board of directors** gave a short statement to the press.

11. **The hideout belonging to the thieves** was raided by the police after they received a tip-off.

12. **The instinct of the mother cats** is to protect their kittens from harm.

 ISBN 978-81-8477-751-2

4 Nouns: Phrases and Clauses

Grammar Help

A **noun phrase** does the work of a noun.
- To find a noun phrase, ask "What?" after the verb.
- A noun phrase has no **finite verb** (a verb that shows the tense; for example **told, says**), but it might contain parts of a verb.
- A noun phrase is not a complete message on its own. It can come before the verb or after the verb.

A *Circle the verb in each sentence and underline the noun phrase.*

1. I cannot remember my new phone number.
2. Exercising in hot weather is foolish.
3. The latest computer is very fast and easy to use.
4. I have written down the name of the book.
5. The time of the television programme was 8:00 pm.
6. Have you heard about John's good fortune?
7. The photo of my aunt on holidays was very clear.
8. The detective placed the time of the murder at about 3:00 am.

B *Add a noun phrase to complete these sentences.*

1. I have enjoyed ______________________________.
2. ______________________________ is not a very nice thing to do.
3. ______________________________ is my favourite leisure time activity.
4. My friends prefer ______________________________.
5. All the students joined in ______________________________.
6. He was exhausted after ______________________________.
7. ______________________________ can be quite difficult to achieve.

 ISBN 978-81-8477-751-2

Grammar Help

A noun phrase can help to make your meaning clearer by telling which noun you mean. For example: *Robin, **my best friend**, likes to read.* This is called **apposition**. Noun phrases in apposition explain the previous noun.

C ***This passage is from a travel article. Underline at least five noun phrases and circle at least five noun phrases in apposition.***

A Trip to Paris

Paris, the capital city of France, is noted for its loveliness, its museums, its art galleries and its nightlife. Everywhere you travel in Paris, you will find something of beauty, such as the bridges that span the River Seine. The waters of the Seine divide the city into two—the left bank and the right bank.

If you visit Paris you will want to see some of its most famous landmarks. The cathedral of Notre Dame, one of the most attractive of the French buildings, is situated in the centre of the city—the river island of Île de la Cité. The Eiffel Tower, another monument of great appeal, dominates the skyline at Champs de Mars, while the Louvre, once a royal palace, has a huge glass prism in its courtyard. The *Mona Lisa,* Leonardo da Vinci's most famous painting, is housed in the Louvre. While these are all very beautiful, my most favourite place in the whole of Paris is a white church, the Sacre Coeur, situated on a hill behind the Louvre.

 ISBN 978-81-8477-751-2

Grammar Help

A **noun clause** also does the work of a noun.

- A noun clause may have a **subject** and it usually has a **finite verb**. It sometimes makes sense on its own.
- A noun clause can come before the main verb or after the main verb.

D ***Use suitable noun clauses from the box to complete the following passage.***

they would fall to the valley below
they would be buried in mud
nobody had been there before
the edge of the ridge was slippery
the danger that lurked over the top of the ridge
what was on the other side
what had happened to them
rain had caused a mud slide

As they drew close to the top of the mountain, the climbers tried to guess (1) ________________________.

This was because (2) ________________________.

They didn't know of (3) ________________________.

The problem was (4) ________________________.

If they were not careful, (5) ________________________ ________________________. Nobody would know (6) ________________________ because (7) ________________________. Luckily the leader noticed (8) ________________________ ________________________. He warned them to proceed very carefully.

 ISBN 978-81-8477-751-2

Grammar Help

A noun clause can also help to make your meaning clearer by telling which one you mean. For example: *Robert, **the boy who lives down the road,** likes to read.* This is called **apposition**. Noun clauses in apposition explain the previous noun.

E ***Add a noun clause from the box below to explain which one you mean.***

that the Earth is round
the one you skidded at yesterday
that the thief was guilty
that a tomato is a vegetable
the one visiting him from Africa
the boy wearing the green T-shirt
the one who scores the most goals
the one you hear barking every night
the very old man who lives near me
the teacher who is most popular with all students
that man walked the Earth thousands of years ago
that you helped the old lady cross the street

1. The dog, ______________________________, is a nuisance.
2. The player, ______________________________, will receive an award.
3. The verdict ______________________________, pleased the victim.
4. The fact ______________________________, shows you are kind.
5. It is beyond doubt ______________________________.

 ISBN 978-81-8477-751-2

6. My son, ____,
won his race at the carnival.

7. James' uncle, ____,
brought him a spear.

8. It is not true ____.

9. The proof ____,
was discovered by archaeologists.

10. Mr Brown, ____,
is always joking with the class.

11. The corner, ____,
is very dangerous.

12. Mr Johnston, ____,
has arthritis.

F ***Read the nonsense poem and underline six noun clauses or phrases. Write "P" above it to show it is a phrase and "C" to show it is a clause.***

Have you heard what happened to the Man in the Moon?

He tried to bully the dish and the spoon.

The cow told him crossly it was not very nice;

To continue would mean he must pay the price.

The punishment for not saying, "Please"

Is to change forever into smelly green cheese.

But the moon just continued his bullying ways

And was turned into cheese for the rest of his days.

 ISBN 978-81-8477-751-2

5 Adjectival Phrases and Clauses

Grammar Help

An **adjectival phrase** is a group of words that acts as an adjective in a sentence. Phrases don't have verbs, so they don't form complete sentences. For example: *happy and contented.*

- Adjectival phrases that come before a noun are often joined with a hyphen. For example: *a* ***three-year*** *savings plan.*
- An adjectival phrase answers the following questions about the noun: *which one? what kind? with what? like what? whose? where? about what?*
- An adjectival phrase may begin with a preposition, but because it is doing the job of describing a noun, it is called an adjectival phrase.

A ***Read this personal recount, and circle the common nouns. Identify the phrase that answers the question e.g. "Which one?" about the noun. Underline the adjectival phrases.***

Last week, our old and outdated computer stopped working, so Dad took us to the computer shop next to the bank to see if it could be repaired. The efficient and friendly sales assistant who served us said that repairing obsolete and outmoded computers is expensive. He suggested we buy an up-to-date and user-friendly model instead. Dad chose the laptop on the counter because he said it had an easy-to-use keyboard. Also, there was a three-week wait for the other one he liked. The boys in my school will be envious when they see our new computer.

 ISBN 978-81-8477-751-2

B ***Complete these definitions by adding an adjectival phrase beginning with "with". The first one shows you how.***

1. Vertebrates are animals with backbones.
2. Insects are animals ______
3. Arachnids are animals ______
4. Marsupials are animals ______
5. Invertebrates are animals ______

C ***Read the adjectival phrases below and write sentences for six of them. Remember that your phrase must describe a noun. The example shows you how.***

of ancient Rome	**without sunglasses**	**next door**
about life in space	**smartly dressed**	**from Japan**
in the middle	**with messy hair**	

1. Aquaducts were an invention of ancient Rome.
2. ______
3. ______
4. ______
5. ______
6. ______
7. ______
8. ______

 ISBN 978-81-8477-751-2

Grammar Help

You can also use **adjectival clauses** to indicate which one. Unlike adjectival phrases, adjectival clauses contain a verb.

Adjectival clauses often begin with a relative pronoun, such as **who, whom, whose, which** and **that**; or with relative adverbs, such as **where, when** and **why**. Thus they are sometimes called **relative clauses**.

D ***Complete each definition with an adjectival clause beginning with who or where.***

1. A geologist is a person ______________________________
2. A stevedore is a person ______________________________
3. A martyr is a person ______________________________
4. An optimist is a person ______________________________
5. An abattoir is a place ______________________________
6. A monastery is a place ______________________________
7. A silo is a place ______________________________
8. An apiary is a place ______________________________

E ***Underline the adjectival clause in each sentence, then rewrite the sentence substituting an adjectival clause of your own.***

1. This is the theatre where I lost my purse.

   ____

2. John bought the book that Sue recommended.

   ____

3. Jack is the basketball player for whom the coach has the most respect.

   ____

4. This is the reason why people cannot breathe in water.

   ____

 ISBN 978-81-8477-751-2

5. Spring is the season when plants begin to grow.

6. Over there is the school where my parents studied.

7. The happy girl, whose story won the prize, celebrated with her friends.

8. The puppy, which had followed Anne home from school, belonged to Jenny.

9. The man who is wearing a white hat is a famous concert pianist.

10. The hospital where I was born in has been renovated a great deal.

Grammar Help

We can shorten some **adjectival clauses** by leaving off the relative pronouns or relative adverbs. Sometimes, we can leave out other words too. For example:
The hospital where I was born in. → *The hospital I was born in.*
My aunt is the woman who is wearing a white dress. → *My aunt is the woman wearing a white dress.*

F ***Shorten five of the sentences from Exercise E by leaving out the relative pronoun or adverb. Choose carefully, there are a couple of tricky ones. Write your shortened sentences here.***

 ISBN 978-81-8477-751-2

6 Adverbials of Time and Reason

Grammar Help

Adverbs and **adverbial phrases of time** tell **when** and often include prepositions.

In a sentence, adverbial phrases of time usually follow the object or a verb. However, they can go in front of a sentence to give it some variety.

A ***Read this letter and underline ten adverbial phrases of time. Circle the prepositions. The first one is done for you.***

Dear Grandma,

Sam and I are having a great time in Disneyland (at) the moment. Thank you so much for the tickets you gave us on our birthdays.

It was raining on the first day, so we stayed inside most of the time. About three o'clock in the afternoon, the sun came out and we made our first visit to Disneyland. The fireworks at night were spectacular. On the following day, we explored the whole theme park, but we didn't get to go on all the rides. Tomorrow morning, we will be going back to try out the rides we missed.

Mum says in a week's time, we'll be going to San Diego to see the Zoo. Do you remember when you took us to the Singapore Zoo at Christmas time last year? I hope we have as much fun in San Diego as we did last December.

We will be arriving home on Saturday, two weeks from today. I can't wait to see you and show you the photos I took on our holiday.

Lots of love,

Su-Lin

 ISBN 978-81-8477-751-2

B ***A proverb is an old, wise saying. Complete these proverbs using adverbs of time from the box. Some of the adverbs will need to be used more than once.***

early	**while**	**twice**	**soon**	**tomorrow**
today	**before**	**once**	**late**	**never**

1. ____________________ to bed and ____________________ to rise, makes a man healthy, wealthy and wise.
2. Do not put off until ____________________ what you can do ____________________ .
3. Don't count your chickens ____________________ they are hatched.
4. A fool and his money are ____________________ parted.
5. ____________________ bitten, ____________________ shy.
6. Look ____________________ you leap.
7. Better ____________________ than ____________________ .
8. Make hay ____________________ the sun shines.

Grammar Help

Adverbs also answer questions about **how often** (frequency) and **how long** (duration) someone does something.

C ***Look at the adverbials in the table below. Use them to fill in the blanks in the extract on the next page, which is the beginning of a story.***

Time (when?)	Frequency (how often?)	Duration (how long?)
instantly last week in the evenings	now and again hardly ever every evening every day from time to time	since that Monday for a whole week now

 ISBN 978-81-8477-751-2

The twins were very upset and couldn't sleep. They had said goodnight to their parents at nine o'clock, as they did (1) ________________________,

but at ten they were still wide-awake and tossing from side to side—over and over again. (2) ________________________, one of the boys would let out a long sigh that was echoed almost (3) ________________________ by his twin brother.

Before that awful Monday (4) ________________________, neither boy had a care in the world; all that had changed in an instant. They had (5) ________________________ had to worry about a thing, but (6) ________________________, they had been burdened by a most important secret. (7) ________________________ they had been tempted to tell someone about it, but whenever this happened, the consequences loomed before them.

(8) ________________________ the burden seemed to grow larger and more worrisome. In fact, the boys could think of nothing else. Each time the teacher spoke to either of them, the question had to be repeated. They used to watch television (9) ________________________ with their parents, but things were not like before. (10) ________________________ the television had been ignored as the twins grappled with their problem.

 ISBN 978-81-8477-751-2

D ***Read the newspaper article below. Can you find at least two each of the different types of adverbs—of place, time, manner, frequency and duration? Fill them in below.***

Soccer Coach Demotes Top Players

Greentown, UK

The team line-up for Saturday's game here changed dramatically overnight as Rover's coach, Ted Long, who is often criticized for rarely changing his team, dumped five of his star players.

"As a rule, I choose players on a yearly basis and seldom alter my opinion. I still believe that players need assurance of the coach's faith in them," explained the unhappy coach defensively; "but players have been taking advantage of this. For example, Brown often comes late for training, Green rarely completes his track work, and I have dropped White permanently because he never attends training held outdoors."

Other players that have been axed include Tan, who is suspended temporarily, and Black, whose position is forfeit until he regains his fitness. It remains to be seen how the Rovers will perform during the match tomorrow. Sometimes a shake-up like this works wonders.

1. Adverbs of place : ______________________ ______________________
2. Adverbs of time : ______________________ ______________________
3. Adverbs of manner : ______________________ ______________________
4. Adverbs of frequency: ______________________ ______________________
5. Adverbs of duration : ______________________ ______________________

 ISBN 978-81-8477-751-2

E ***Complete the following, using the given adverbials of reason to help you make a suitable sentence.***

1. Because of his disobedience, Jack ______________________________

______________________________.

2. Due to her brave efforts ______________________________

______________________________.

3. ______________________________

through bad planning.

4. ______________________________

from old age.

5. ______________________________

because of the stormy weather.

6. As a result of his kindness ______________________________

______________________________.

7. Because of the accident ______________________________

______________________________.

8. In view of your good work, ______________________________

______________________________.

9. Because of her stupidity, ______________________________

______________________________.

10. ______________________________

through their fine efforts.

 ISBN 978-81-8477-751-2

7 Adverbs of Degree

Grammar Help

Adverbs of degree tell us how much or to what degree an action is done. They answer the question: "To what extent?"

They usually go before verbs, and sometimes adjectives or adverbs. For example: *I **barely** know Mr Lang. I am **fairly** certain I locked the door.* But there are a few exceptions: *He ran quickly **enough** to catch the train. I turned up the oven **a little**.*

A ***Complete the following statements by adding the most suitable adverb of degree from the box for each blank.***

quite	hardly	partially	rather
partly	nearly	almost	much

1. My grandfather is always saying that things were ______________ better in the past.
2. "Speak up. I can ______________ hear you," yelled the old lady.
3. "Please wait," Sally begged, "I've ______________ completed my homework. I just have to write two more sentences."
4. "When I came out of the shop, my car was ______________ covered in paint," complained the customer.
5. "This is an improvement on your last test. I'm ______________ pleased with you, but I know you can do better," stated the teacher.
6. "I've ______________ finished knitting the sweater; I only have to complete the sleeves," reported Grandmother.
7. The motorist offered: "Let me fix the bike for you—it's only ______________ broken. It just needs a new front wheel and lamp."
8. "I'm ______________ busy at the moment. Could I call you back in about fifteen minutes?" Mr James said while scribbling his report.

 ISBN 978-81-8477-751-2

Grammar Help

Intensifiers are a special group of adverbs of degree used to 'strengthen' the meaning of the adjective or adverb after them. They can also intensify verbs and nouns. For example: *John is **very** clever (**indeed**) with his hands. In the past, Conrad's books were **much** admired. I am **such** a coward about pain.*

Many intensifiers are **-ly** adverbs. For example: *He felt **deeply** hurt by the betrayal.*

B ***Read the newspaper headlines below. All of them have adverbs in them. Mark those that use an adverb of degree or an intensifier with a cross in the boxes. Underline the adverb of degree or the intensifier.***

1. Man almost killed by tiger ☐
2. Farmhouse totally destroyed by fire ☐
3. Donations of rice to be airlifted immediately ☐
4. Weather rather warm for winter says Met Service ☐
5. Manager admits football fans behaved very badly ☐
6. Space travel soon possible for everyone ☐
7. Young mother seriously injured in car crash ☐
8. Trade figures slightly lower than last year ☐
9. Police completely outnumbered in riot ☐
10. Government now admits grave error ☐
11. Villagers claim extinct animal still exists ☐
12. Government never considers the poor ☐
13. Palace officials say Princess is "much better" ☐

 ISBN 978-81-8477-751-2

C ***The phrases in the box contain adverbs of degree or intensifiers. Complete the passage by filling in each blank with a suitable phrase.***

almost drowned	**exceptionally fast**
quite poor	**very contented**
rather different	**extremely brave**
nearly finished	**really lucky**
just about read	**particularly boring**
fairly heavy	**totally submerged**
too much	**unusually thin**
far prefer	**pretty wealthy**

My friend John and I are (1) rather different. For a start, John is interested in reading historical novels, but I find them (2) ____________. Also, he has (3) ____________ all the books in the school library. On weekends, I (4) ____________ to laze around instead of attending to my books. John, on the other hand, will have (5) ____________ all his homework by Saturday.

There are other differences too. I can afford to buy a lot of computer games because my family is (6) ____________. John does without a lot of luxuries as his family is (7) ____________. However, he is (8) ____________ to go without computer games as long as he can visit the library every day.

I think John is a hero. Once, I fell in and (9) ____________ in a river that was flowing (10) ____________; John jumped in to save me. This was (11) ____________ of him because he is an (12) ____________ boy, while I, being well fed, am (13) ____________. Still John managed to keep me from being (14) ____________ in the swirling water until help arrived. I think I am (15) ____________ to have such a fantastic friend.

 ISBN 978-81-8477-751-2

D ***Now answer the questions about the passage. Use an intensifier or an adverb of degree in your answer.***

1. What evidence is there in the passage that John is a very good student?

____

____

2. What evidence is there in the passage that suggests John reads almost every night?

____

____

3. What evidence is there in the passage that tells you the writer is a bit lazy?

____

____

4. Why couldn't John buy computer games?

____

____

5. Why did the writer say that John was a hero?

____

____

6. What made it harder for John to save the writer?

____

____

7. What evidence is there to suggest that John was in danger when he was trying to rescue the writer?

____

____

8. What evidence do you have that the writer values John's friendship?

____

____

 ISBN 978-81-8477-751-2

E ***There are three or four adverbs of degree or intensifiers in each short paragraph below. Underline them.***

1. He was deeply hurt because she had completely forgotten to call him back, despite the fact that she had promised to do so on several occasions. However, he felt much better when she called to apologise the next day.
2. It was the worst game the team had ever played and they had been soundly beaten. The players in the changing room were looking absolutely depressed. However, the coach seemed fairly optimistic that the team would do better next time.
3. Mary thought that it was entirely Jane's own fault. She had hardly studied for the exam despite several reminders from the teacher and her parents. Now she had almost failed an exam that should have been easy for such a talented student.
4. The children have been cooperating rather well these holidays. Jack has almost completed his school project and Jane has partially completed hers. But, Betsy is the star. She has completely finished.
5. I had hardly finished eating my evening meal, when I heard a quite loud rapping on my front door. Upon opening it, I could scarcely believe my eyes.
6. It was a fairly small creature with incredibly blue eyes. Meg had found it down by the nearly empty water tank. It must have been terribly thirsty because it was frantically licking the tiny drips that seeped from the mouth of the leaking tap.

 ISBN 978-81-8477-751-2

8 Present Participles Used as Gerunds

Grammar Help

- Present participles (verbs that end with *–ing*) can be used as nouns. They are called **gerunds** or verbal nouns, for example: ***Skipping*** *is good exercise.*
- Present participles can also be used as adjectives: *He sat at the **dining** table.*

A ***Read this introduction from a report. Circle the present participles (verbs + -ing) that are used as adjectives. Underline the present participles that are used as gerunds.***

The World of Living Things

The world of living things can be grouped according to similarities and differences. Animal scientists do this by studying how members of the animal kingdom are alike. This is not always an easy task. Even within the same group of animals there may be surprising differences. For example, while most mammals are land-living animals, some like the bat are flying creatures. The aquatic mammals, such as the whale and the dolphin, move from place to place by swimming. Others, like the mole, are digging animals that use their burrows for escaping from predators. Therefore the animals' "moving in different ways" is not a very useful method of classifying them. Instead, scientists rely on the classifying of a wider group of features, such as whether the animal has a backbone (vertebrates) or not (invertebrates).

 ISBN 978-81-8477-751-2

B ***Form gerunds from the verbs in the box and use them to complete the sentences below.***

age	**rely**	**race**
swelter	**hike**	**work**
steal	**paint**	**make**
cycle	**pay**	**cheat**
skip	**surf**	**bake**

1. In many countries, ________________ can provide an economical way of moving around.
2. ________________ is exciting, especially if you catch a big wave.
3. Linda is talented in ________________ and has received awards in many art competitions.
4. My friend's hobby is ________________ , so she is going to make a big cake for my birthday.
5. He was accused of ________________ in the examination.
6. ________________ is strenuous on mountain trails.
7. ________________ is easy, but only if your rope is of the correct length.
8. ________________ is a dangerous sport.
9. Settling into a new school involves ________________ new friends.
10. The thief admitted ________________ the priceless painting.
11. The thrifty housewife resented ________________ high prices for branded goods.
12. The independent boy detested ________________ on others.
13. The shift-worker is used to ________________ at night.

 ISBN 978-81-8477-751-2

14. The beautiful film star dreaded ________________ .

15. I can't imagine ________________ at home in summer.

Grammar Help

A gerund can consist of more than one word: it can be a **gerund phrase**. For example: *Boys in the past used to enjoy* ***trainspotting;*** *while girls did* ***flower pressing*** *and* ***scrapbook making.***

C ***Read the clues and match the person to the gerund phrase that represents his or her activity.***

1. Jan doesn't have much money, but she likes nice things. •	• tap dancing
2. Jenny has many penfriends. •	• baby sitting
3. Kim is not afraid of heights. •	• water skiing
4. Mrs Jones likes small children. •	• letter writing
5. Martha frequently visits the craft shop. •	• marathon running
6. Rick has metal tips on his shoes. •	• rock climbing
7. Kate wears a life jacket. •	• paper toling
8. Jack has a lot of stamina. •	• window-shopping

 ISBN 978-81-8477-751-2

D ***Underline the gerund phrases in the sentences below, then use them to decide which piece of equipment in the box belongs has been each blank. Write the equipment in the blank. The first one has been done for you.***

binoculars	**easel**	**parachute**
stopwatch	**sewing kit**	**music stand**
rod and reel	**roller blades**	**helmet**
board and sail	**pump**	

1. I know that Gerard likes skydiving, so this parachute must be his.
2. Mike is keen on deep-sea fishing, so this ______________ belongs to him.
3. Carol likes in-line skating, so these ______________ are hers.
4. Mary is an artist who prefers portrait painting, so this ______________ must be hers.
5. Windsurfing is Ted's favourite activity, so the ______________ must be his.
6. Kim is a nature lover who likes birdwatching, so these ______________ are hers.
7. Jane loves flute playing, so this ______________ must belong to her.
8. Ted said Penny is good at dress-making, so this ______________ must belong to her.
9. Gary goes bike riding at every opportunity, so this ______________ and that ______________ will be his.
10. Angie likes to time her long-distance running, so this ______________ is hers.

 ISBN 978-81-8477-751-2

E ***Read the sentences below. Make new sentences by replacing the infinitive verbs with gerunds. The first one has been done for you.***

1. It is easier to skate on ice than to skate on roller blades.

   Skating on ice is easier than skating on roller blades.

2. It is easier to speak Mandarin than to read it.

   ____

3. To spare the rod means to spoil the child.

   ____

4. To see is to believe.

   ____

5. To run is faster than to jog.

   ____

6. To give is better than to receive.

   ____

7. To err is human but to forgive is divine.

   ____

8. To help others often means to give up your own priorities.

   ____

9. To be a good citizen means to put society's needs before your own.

   ____

   ____

10. To park in the city is more difficult than to find a parking space in a suburban shopping centre.

    ____

    ____

 ISBN 978-81-8477-751-2

9 Phrasal Verbs

Grammar Help

Many English verbs have two parts—a base verb and a preposition or adverb, for example: ***get off, put in for***. They are known as **phrasal verbs**. The preposition or adverb helps to give the verbs different meanings.

A ***Read the personal recount below.***

1. Underline all the phrasal verbs formed from the verb **fall**.

We had been marching despondently for days. Our dreams of a glorious victory had fallen through more than a week ago. The enemy had fallen on us with such ferocity that we could only fall the day we fell back in retreat. I knew some of my companions had fallen behind, and I was worried about them. I also suspected that the commanding officer had no emergency plans to fall back on after he had fallen out with some of the other officers and refused to listen to their advice. The number of men prepared to fight had fallen off. Some of the men refused to fall in, or fall out, when ordered to, and some of the soldiers were tired of falling in with the orders of officers other than their own sergeant.

2. Match some of the phrasal verbs you underlined with their meaning below.

(a) get into ranks ____________________

(b) failed to happen ____________________

 ISBN 978-81-8477-751-2

(c) declined in number ____________________

(d) obeying ____________________

(e) attacked unexpectedly ____________________

(f) quarrelled ____________________

B ***These sentences are missing phrasal verbs. Choose the most suitable one from the box for each sentence.***

depends on	**put away**
burnt down	**calls for**
blew up	**disapproves of**
ran out of	**moved out of**
turn down	**carried out**

1. My teacher ____________________ laziness.
2. She ____________________ her mother to do everything for her.
3. The rebels ____________________ the railway.
4. You must ____________________ your toys.
5. She quickly ____________________ ideas.
6. The bushfire ____________________ the farmhouse.
7. Your success ____________________ a celebration.
8. The tenant ____________________ the house.
9. Sally is proud and will ____________________ offers of help.
10. They ____________________ the task on time.

 ISBN 978-81-8477-751-2

C *In the following conversation, the phrasal verbs are in bold print. Match each phrasal verb with its meaning given in the box by writing the letter of the meaning in the small square after the phrasal verb.*

a. require	**b. telephone**
c. greet from a distance	**d. visit to collect**
e. visit a place	**f. visit expecting to stay briefly**
g. visit briefly	**h. cancel**

Henry and Bill see their football coach approaching and they (1) **call out** ☐ *to him.*

Henry & Bill : Hi, Coach!

Coach : Hello, Henry and Bill. Have you seen Fred? I (2) **call out** ☐ his house, but he wasn't home.

Bill : We (3) **called for** ☐ him too, but his mother said he had already left with John to play football. We had arranged to (4) **call in at** ☐ Tom's first, and then go for a film show.

Henry : Why did you (5) **call on** ☐ him, Coach?

Coach : I was going to (6) **call off** ☐ the football match because it looks like it will rain.

Henry : That (7) **calls for** ☐ action. Why don't you (8) **call up** ☐ Fred on his mobile phone? That's what we always do.

Coach : Great! That's just what I'll do. I'll call him now.

 ISBN 978-81-8477-751-2

D ***Many phrasal verbs can be formed from "break". The box shows five.***

1. Match the phrasal verbs in the first column with their meaning in the second column. Write the letter of the meaning in the brackets after the phrasal verb.

break down ( )	**a.**	**terminate or end suddenly**
break out ( )	**b.**	**overcome**
break through ( )	**c.**	**enter by force**
break into ( )	**d.**	**start suddenly**
break off ( )	**e.**	**become very bad or come to an end**

2. Complete this news report by filling in the blanks with suitable phrasal verbs from the box above. You may have to change the tense form.

Someone (a) ____________________ an office at the Romanian Embassy in Prague last night. This has caused relationships to (b) ____________________ between Hungary and Romania. The incident has also prompted the two countries to (c) ____________________ trading arrangements reached at the last meeting between their Trade Ministers. Analysts fear that war could (d) ____________________ if the countries involved can't (e) ____________________ the deadlock this has caused.

 ISBN 978-81-8477-751-2

10 Modals: used to, need, dare

Grammar Help

Modal verbs such as **used to** and **would** can be used to talk about habits in the past.

- **Used to** and **would** can be used interchangeably except with stative verbs (which talk about feelings and thoughts), as well as **be** and **have** (= possess). You cannot use **would** in such sentences. For example: *John* ***used to be*** *my best friend.* (not **would be**) *Grandfather* ***used to have*** *a younger brother.* (not **would have**) *I* ***used to think*** *that Santa Claus was a real person.* (not **would think**)
- To talk about regular habits, you should include adverbs of time, such as **each time, whenever** or **every time**.

A ***The following passage describes what life was like for women in ancient Greece. Rewrite the numbered sentences in the passage using*** **used to** ***or*** **would** ***to express habits in the past. You will need to change the underlined verbs as well.***

Women in ancient Greece <u>experience</u> a busy, but stress-free life. (1) Every day, they arise early to fetch water from the well because there <u>is</u> no plumbing in the house. (2) Then they prepare food for later, before saying their prayers. (3) Mid morning <u>is</u> also a busy time during which the women put on their veils and go with their slaves to the market to buy food for the next day. (4) By midday, everyone <u>is</u> hungry, so the women serve the food they <u>have</u> cooked in the morning. (5) Some women spend the afternoon spinning. Others <u>prefer</u> to sew. (6) However, all of them bathe before the evening meal. (7) This meal <u>is</u> a communal occasion which some relations join the family for. (8) Friends arrive later for a social gathering. (9) Rich families entertain lavishly. (10) They hire professional entertainers like dancers and musicians.

 ISBN 978-81-8477-751-2

B ***You are telling stories to some friends of the time when you were younger, before you started going to primary school. Write 5 sentences of what you used to do then. For example: I used to visit my grandmother every Sunday.***

1. ____________________

2. ____________________

3. ____________________

 ISBN 978-81-8477-751-2

4. ____

____

5. ____

____

Grammar Help

- To express doubt, necessity or responsibility, you can use the modal **need**. For example: *Do you **need** to train so hard for the match? We all **need** not worry about that yet.*
- The modal **can** is used to talk about ability, while **will** is used to express intention.

C ***Everyone has responsibility towards others. Using the modals provided, complete the following sentences to describe how you can help out in the given situations. The first one is done as an example.***

Within your family

1. I should help clean up the house because both my parents work very long hours and they get tired.

2. I must ____

____

3. I will ____

____

4. I should not ____

____

5. I need ____

____

 ISBN 978-81-8477-751-2

Within your classroom and school

6. I must not ____

____

7. I need ____

____

8. I will ____

____

9. I can ____

____

10. I should ____

____

Within your group of friends and community

11. I must ____

____

12. I should not ____

____

13. I need ____

____

14. I will ____

____

15. I can ____

____

 ISBN 978-81-8477-751-2

Grammar Help

To express anger or annoyance, you can use the modal **dare**. For example: *Don't you **dare** read my personal letters.*

D ***Read the following statements that use dare to express anger or disapproval. For each of the statements, write a second sentence that tells what the subject needs to do instead. An example is provided to help you.***

1. How dare you copy Tim's work.

   You need to study harder so that you can do the work yourself.

2. Don't you dare run across a busy road like that again.

   ____

   ____

3. I was first—how dare you push in front of me.

   ____

   ____

4. How dare you enter the Principal's office without any permission.

   ____

   ____

5. I don't mind lending you my bike, but don't you dare just take it.

   ____

   ____

6. How dare you speak to your grandma like that.

   ____

   ____

7. Don't you dare bully the younger pupils in school.

   ____

   ____

 ISBN 978-81-8477-751-2

11 Different Kinds of Verbs

Grammar Help

- **Action verbs** tell you about physical actions, for example: ***fall, work, bark***.
- **"Saying" verbs** tell you how characters speak, for example: *"Stop right there!"* ***commanded*** *the policeman.*
- **Stative verbs** tell about a state or condition. They show the relationship between things or show how a person feels about or sees things; that is, they indicate beliefs and opinions. Examples of stative verbs are ***seem, appear, consider, enjoy, dislike, wonder***.

A ***The text below is taken from a narrative which uses many action verbs. Choose the correct verb from the brackets to fill in each blank.***

The children (1) ________________ (raced, cried) excitedly down to see the waves that (2) ________________ (chuckled, crashed) onto the stony foreshore. It was a perfect day for the start of the holidays. Small crabs (3) ________________ (skittered, danced) about on the rocks as the swirling foam (4) ________________ (eddied, swayed), and seagulls (5) ________________ (fluttered, swooped) and (6) ________________ (dived, searched), hoping for an easy meal.

When the children reached the water's edge, they (7) ________________ (cried, hesitated) for a while. They (8) ________________ (stopped, watched) as the water (9) ________________ (swallowed, sucked) and (10) ________________ (turned, swirled) again and again, depositing and dragging shells backwards and forwards with every movement. They tentatively (11) ________________ (ran, waded) into the blue sea. A chilly wind (12) ________________ (arose, came) but the sun (13) ________________ (blasted, beamed) at the children, warming their pale skin and turning it golden.

 ISBN 978-81-8477-751-2

B ***Complete each sentence with a suitable action verb from the box. Use each verb only once.***

ransacked	lurked	persevered	swaggered
dramatized	languished	rampaged	defied

1. The arrogant boy ________________ past the people in the queue.
2. He ________________ in the shadows, watching every movement the old man made.
3. The soldiers ________________ through the village, looting the shops and breaking people's furniture.
4. He ________________ after his wife's death, as he missed her terribly.
5. She boldly ________________ her parents' wishes.
6. The witness ________________ the whole incident vividly.
7. The burglars ________________ the house in search of valuables.
8. Despite the difficulties, he ________________ with the problem.

C ***Circle the correct verb to use in these sentences.***

1. If you wish to (ensure / insure / assure) that you will always have somewhere to live, you must (ensure / insure / assure) your house.
2. She (bought / brought) the painting that I had (bought / brought) to be auctioned at the charity sale.
3. At the same time they decided to (emigrate / immigrate) to Australia, their friends decided to (emigrate / immigrate) from China to Canada.
4. Can you (devise / device) something that will help me open this door.
5. The old man (pedalled / peddled) his bicycle down the street, then (pedalled / peddled) his goods at the corner.
6. The dressmaker promised to (cloth / clothe) the princess in the finest silk in the land.

 ISBN 978-81-8477-751-2

D ***Below is a dialogue in a narrative text. Choose the more suitable saying verbs to complete the text.***

Jane had never really liked May, and now the dislike had come to the fore. Jane's beautiful costumed doll lay headless on the ground.

"Please forgive me," (1) ________________ (pleaded, said) May. "It was an accident. Really!"

"I don't believe you. Your mother will be so angry when she finds out you broke my expensive doll," (2) ________________ (smirked, consoled) Jane. "Of course, you meant to do it. You're too poor to own a doll like mine," she (3) ________________ (warned, sneered), "so you broke mine just because you're jealous."

"No, no!" May (4) ________________ (repeated, protested). "It wasn't like that at all. I only wanted to hold it, but you grabbed it back so quickly, the head came off. Please, Jane, you are so lucky to have such a beautiful doll. I would do anything to make it whole again," she (5) ________________ (wailed, pleaded) tearfully.

"Would you eat a cup of worms?" (6) ________________ (challenged, demanded) Jane.

"A cup of w-w-worms? Only if it would stop you from telling my mum. I suppose so," May (7) ________________ (agreed, whispered) reluctantly, "just as long as you don't say a word."

"Well, if you will do that, I won't tell her," Jane (8) ________________ (chuckled, assured) May.

Just then Jane's mother appeared from the house. "I heard that, Jane. How could you treat your friend so meanly? Apologise at once and go to your room," she (9) ________________ (scolded, growled).

"I'm sorry, May, for being mean to you," Jane (10) ________________ (apologized, remarked) and turned to go. She realized she had been very unkind. She hoped that May would forgive her, and maybe they could be true friends.

 ISBN 978-81-8477-751-2

E ***Use a stative verb from the box to fill in each blank. Remember that stative verbs are words that tell about feelings, thoughts, beliefs and opinions.***

wonder	**realize**	**enjoy**	**hate**
understand	**think**	**need**	**fear**
dislike	**please**	**adore**	**feel**

In today's paper, I read that some people (1) ________________ animals and actually hurt them. I (2) ________________ animals and cannot (3) ________________ how anyone could injure a dog or a cat. I (4) ________________ why these people have pets in the first place if they do not (5) ________________ looking after animals. Perhaps they (6) ________________ a pet will amuse them. Or they buy one to (7) ________________ other people and then (8) ________________ that they (9) ________________ the responsibility of owning a pet. People like this (10) ________________ to remember that animals have feelings too.

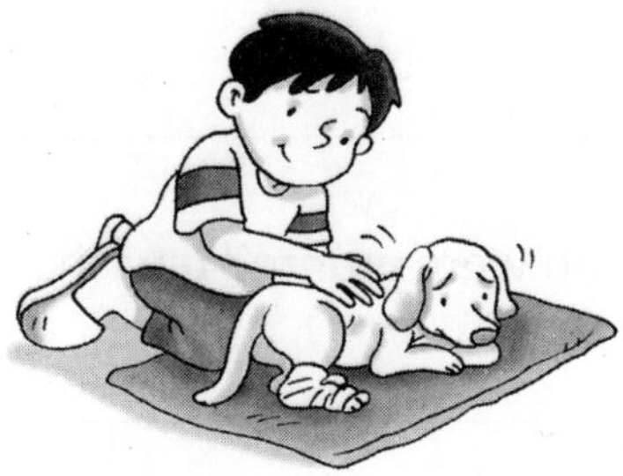

F ***Read the following directions and respond to them. Note that the words in bold print are stative verbs. Write your answers in complete sentences using the stative verbs as shown in the examples.***

Examples: Name two things that you **despise**.

I despise ill treatment of animals.

I despise rude people.

 ISBN 978-81-8477-751-2

1. Write two things that you **remember** about your first day at school.

____

____

2. Write about two things that **frighten** you.

____

____

3. What are two things that **amuse** you?

____

____

4. What kind of a pet would you **love** to own?

____

____

5. If you were granted a wish, what would you **wish** to own?

____

____

 ISBN 978-81-8477-751-2

12 Simple Past and Past Continuous Tenses

Grammar Help

- You use the simple past tense for actions that happened in the past and to report completed actions. This tense is used a lot in recounts and narratives. For example: *The movie* ***started*** *at 6:00 pm. We* ***were overjoyed*** *that our team* ***won*** *both matches. Two people* ***died*** *in the flash floods.*
- Past tense verbs are used to indicate past habits or repeated events that are now over. For example: *As a teenager, my father* ***was*** *always the tallest boy in his class. I always* ***rode*** *a bike to school when I was young.*
- An adverb of frequency is often used to show that a simple past tense verb is describing a habit.

A ***The past tense is often used in newspaper reports. Some of the verbs in the following report are missing. Change the present tense verbs in the box to past tense. Then use them to complete the newspaper report.***

run ______	**see** ______	**treat** ______
save ______	**take** ______	**fall** ______
trip ______	**pull** ______	**hold** ______
try ______	**praise** ______	**leap** ______
send ______	**perform** ______	**suffer** ______

Eleven-year-old John Parker from Green Street School

(1) ______________ a stunning rescue yesterday when he

(2) ______________ a small boy from drowning in a fast-flowing

drain.

 ISBN 978-81-8477-751-2

Sam Brown's mother was on her way home with her son when the toddler suddenly (3) __________________ away from her to chase his toy. He (4) __________________ and (5) __________________ into the drain when he (6) __________________ to retrieve his ball, which had rolled into the drain. Fortunately, John (7) __________________ the accident. Without hesitation, he (8) __________________ into the water. He (9) __________________ onto the boy until bystanders (10) __________________ them both out of the water.

Little Sam (11) __________________ no more than a grazed knee, but ambulance officers (12) __________________ his mother for shock. They (13) __________________ her to hospital, where she was admitted for further observation. Officers (14) __________________ John Parker for his actions and they (15) __________________ him home in a squad car.

 ISBN 978-81-8477-751-2

B ***Read the following recount that describes Mr Potts' and the writer's past habits. Write at least ten past habits in the spaces provided on the next page and underline the past tense verbs in your answers. The first one has been done for you.***

Memories of Mr Potts

I will never forget my neighbour, old Mr Potts. Although he was stooped and walked with a stick, he shuffled to the park every afternoon at three o'clock and watched the children playing.

His habits were very predictable. He regularly stopped at the newsagent. That was why he always carried a newspaper under his arm when he arrived at the park. He also bought sweets every day and kept these in a tattered old shopping bag. He consistently gave them to children who showed sportsmanship. Whenever Mr Potts appeared, we always ran over and greeted him with a smile. After he had said hello, he frequently sat on the bench and talked to us. I carried his bag home for him almost every day because he lived next to me. Before he entered his garden, he looked in his letterbox, but there were never any letters. Then he called out to his cat. It usually waited on the step. He often let me feed the cat for him and I loved stroking its soft fur every day. Each night, I filled the cat's dish with warm milk. I was really sorry when Mr Potts left to live with his daughter.

 ISBN 978-81-8477-751-2

1. Mr Potts shuffled to the park every afternoon at three o'clock.

 ISBN 978-81-8477-751-2

Grammar Help

You use a simple past tense verb after the word **wish**. For example: *I wish I **had** a baby sister. I wish I **didn't have** to go to school. I wish I **weren't** feeling so full.*

C ***Here is a list of things that people often wish for. Write sentences like the one given below. Be sure to add why you wish for it.***

1. **wings**
2. **lots of money**
3. **live in U.S.A.**
4. **own a new video game**
5. **lots of friends**
6. **don't have to study**

1. I wish I had wings. Then I'd fly above the treetops and across the mountains.

2. ______________________________

3. ______________________________

4. ______________________________

5. ______________________________

6. ______________________________

 ISBN 978-81-8477-751-2

Grammar Help

- The past continuous tense is used when an ongoing action in the past is interrupted by another one. For example: *When he opened his eyes, he saw all his friends* ***were waiting*** *to welcome him home.*
- The past continuous is also used for an action that was going on at a given period or period of time in the past. For example: *While Jack* ***was filling*** *in the hole, his dog* ***was digging*** *another one.*
- The tense is often used with words like **when**, **while**, and **as**.

D ***Read the following sentences that describe what happened to Tony. For each sentence, fill in the past continuous form or the simple past form of the given verbs to show that an ongoing action was interrupted by another action in the past.***

1. I ________________ (stand) in the aisle of a crowded bus on my way to the office when suddenly someone ________________ (jostle) me.

2. He ________________ (squeeze) past me just as the door ________________ (open) to let another passenger off.

 ISBN 978-81-8477-751-2

3. Because I was off-balance, I ____________________ (fall) out of the bus as the doors ____________________ (close).

4. Then, while I ____________________ (struggle) to get up, it ____________________ (start) to rain heavily. I decided to run to the nearest taxi stand.

5. As I ____________________ (run) in the rain, a huge dog ____________________ (begin) to chase me. So I headed for a nearby tree.

6. While I ____________________ (climb) the tree to escape the dog, I ____________________ (slip), landed awkwardly and ____________________ (break) my ankle.

7. The ride to the hospital ____________________ (take) ages, as the ambulance ____________________ (skid) all over the wet road.

8. The driver ____________________ (cope) marvellously, but I ____________________ (shiver) from the cold.

9. At the hospital, everyone ____________________ (run) around frantically, then someone ____________________ (bump) into my gurney.

   I was knocked onto the floor and cracked my arm. I should have known—it was Friday the thirteenth.

 ISBN 978-81-8477-751-2

13 Present Perfect Tense

Grammar Help

- The **present perfect tense** is used to talk about an action that happened some time before now. You use the simple past tense when you talk about an action that happened at a *definite* time in the past.
- The present perfect tense shows how a past situation relates to the present. For example: ***I've done*** *my homework, so I can help you with yours now.*
- The present perfect tense is also used to talk about actions that started in the past until now and possibly into the future. For example: *I* ***have used*** *this brand of soap always.*
- To form the present perfect tense, you use ***have*** or ***has*** + **past participle**, for example, *I* ***have missed*** *my train. She* ***has completed*** *her homework.*

A ***Read the advertisement below and underline all the present perfect tense verbs.***

University student wanted for part-time gardening work

A family who has lived in the Hillview Park area for twenty years requires the services of a strong, enthusiastic university student who likes gardening. The owner of the garden has suffered a stroke.

Someone who has studied horticulture is preferred, as the owner has planted many exotic and rare plants that need special care.

The rate of pay is $20 per hour, but applicants who have had experience in caring for exotic plants may be paid higher.

Please call **360 7559**, *if you are interested.*

 ISBN 978-81-8477-751-2

B ***John has applied for the advertised job in Exercise A and Mr Hobson is interviewing him. Complete the interview with suitable present perfect tense form of the verbs in the box. The first one has been done for you.***

choose	be	work	have
convince	want	show	start

Mr Hobson : Thank you for answering my advertisement, John. You seem very young. (1) ___Have___ you ___worked___ as a gardener, before?

John : No, but I (2) ______________ an interest in gardening since I was a very young child.

Mr Hobson : What made you so interested in plants?

John : My grandfather loves gardening and he (3) ______________ me how to look after many kinds of orchids. I love exotic plants too. That's why I (4) ______________ to study horticulture, instead of biology.

Mr Hobson : How long have you been studying horticulture then?

John : I (5) ______________ just ______________ university and so (6) ______________ on the course for only about three months.

Mr Hobson : What made you apply for this job? What are your plans for the future?

John : I (7) ______________ always ______________ to work at a large botanical garden and I thought this work would give me some practical experience.

Mr Hobson : Well, John, you (8) ______________ me that you are the person I'm looking for. I will start you on $20 per hour and after you have worked for me for a couple of months, I'll review your salary.

 ISBN 978-81-8477-751-2

Grammar Help

- The **present perfect tense** is used to talk about previous experiences when the exact time is not important, for example: *I **have played** netball **before**.*
- You use adverbs such as **for, since, never, ever, always, just, yet, already, recently** and **still** when you talk about actions that happened some time in the past until now. For example:

  *He **has just completed** his project.*
  *He **has already completed** his project.*
  *He **still hasn't completed** his project.*
  *He **hasn't yet completed** his project.*
  *He **has always completed** his projects on time.*

C ***Read the following sentences and write what you think has happened. Use the present perfect tense and the adverb given in brackets in your answer. A possible answer is provided for the first one as an example.***

1. The floor is wet. (just)

   The maid has just mopped it.

2. The dishes are dirty and the table is covered in crumbs. (just)

   ____

   ____

3. "You are very disobedient," scolded Mother, looking at the books on the floor. (yet)

   ____

   ____

4. "What a brave girl you are, May, I thought you were afraid of the dentist." (recently)

   ____

   ____

 ISBN 978-81-8477-751-2

5. The new neighbours are unpacking the cartons of books and clothes. (already)

6. Mr Smith is afraid of travelling and never leaves the country. (always)

7. “Look at your room. Mother will be very angry when she sees it.” (still)

8. We can watch our favourite television programme. (already)

9. Thousands of villagers are left homeless and are in urgent need of medical aid and food. (recently)

10. Patrick does not cycle to school although he has a bicycle. (still)

 ISBN 978-81-8477-751-2

D ***You have been interviewing a new singing sensation. Here are her answers to some of your questions. Write out what the questions might have been. Try to use the present perfect tense and the adverb, if any is given.***

1. I never really sang in a musical professionally. We once did *Cats* in school for a fund-raiser. (before)

   ____

   ____

2. I went for a few singing lessons. I had to stop after four months as we could not afford them. (ever)

   ____

   ____

3. The director heard me sing two months ago. I guess you could say I had my audition for the part. (already)

   ____

   ____

 ISBN 978-81-8477-751-2

4. No, I never visited London before. I'm looking forward to flying there. (recently)

____

____

5. No. My manager will give me the playscript as soon as she gets it. Then I will read it. (yet)

____

____

6. The director told me that the musical is based on the life of Anne Frank.

____

____

7. I left school four years ago, when I finished my 'O' Level Exam. (since)

____

____

8. Sometimes I wish I did not stop school, but we needed the money then. Maybe I can take up a diploma course. (ever)

____

____

9. You know, I don't really know how much I earned this year! I'm just glad my manager takes good care of the money.

____

____

10. Yes. Even when I was two, I wanted to be a singer. I never saw myself doing anything else. (always)

____

____

 ISBN 978-81-8477-751-2

14 Present Perfect Continuous Tense

Grammar Help

- The **present perfect continuous** is used to talk about actions that began in the past but continued or are related to the present. For example: ***I have been living*** *in Singapore since 1997. I'm dirty because* ***I've been cleaning*** *the garage.*
- To form the present perfect continuous tense, you use **have/has** + **been** + **present participle**. **Have** and **has** can be contracted, for example: ***I've*** *been feeling quite ill.* ***He's*** *been feeling quite ill.*
- When asking a question in the present perfect continuous, you use **have** + **proper noun/pronoun** + **been** + **present participle**. For example: ***Have you been writing*** *to your grandmother?*

A ***Read the following dialogue and underline the present perfect continuous verbs. The first two have been done for you.***

Doctor : What can I do for you today, Mrs Ross? I hope the new medicine has been working.

Mrs Ross : I thought I should come and see you, Doctor, because I've been feeling very tired lately, even with the new medicine you gave me.

Doctor : That's very strange. Have you noticed any other symptoms?

Mrs Ross : Well, I've been putting on a lot of weight lately, and I'm sure I haven't been eating any more than usual. Also, I've been feeling very ill in the mornings.

Doctor : Have you been suffering from giddiness or shortness of breath as well?

Mrs Ross : Not really, although I have been experiencing trouble sleeping and I've been getting more headaches than usual.

 ISBN 978-81-8477-751-2

Doctor : Have you been taking the new medication regularly?

Mrs Ross : Not always. I have really been trying to remember, but sometimes I get very busy and I forget.

Doctor : You've been exercising, haven't you?

Mrs Ross : Not regularly. Not since I've been working at the school part time.

Doctor : Oh, so you have been teaching at the school again. Perhaps you have been working too hard and ignoring your fitness.

Mrs Ross : I suppose I have been sitting at a desk longer than usual, and I haven't been swimming for a long while since I've been teaching. Perhaps that's the reason.

Doctor : I'll examine you to make sure, but I really think your problems are because you have not been taking your medicine regularly enough and because you have not been exercising the way you used to exercise.

B ***Use the words in brackets to write a possible answer to each question in the present perfect continuous tense. The first one has been done for you.***

1. Why is Jane at night school? (learn, French)

   She has been learning how to speak French.

2. Why hasn't John done his homework? (take, dogs, walk)

   ____

   ____

3. Why did Pat buy you a present? (help, project)

   ____

 ISBN 978-81-8477-751-2

4. Why is Sheila busy on Saturdays? (go, piano lesson)

____

5. Why are you so angry? (wait, four hours)

____

6. How long has Paul been an artist? (paint, since high school)

____

____

7. Why are you two so dirty? (dig, garden)

____

8. Why won't you come with me tonight? (study, exams, tired)

____

____

9. Why isn't Jack home yet? (visit, uncle)

____

10. Why is the dog panting so much? (climb, stairs)

____

____

11. What is that delicious smell? (bake, cakes)

____

12. Why wasn't Jill at school on the first day of term? (touring, France, Grandma)

____

____

 ISBN 978-81-8477-751-2

Grammar Help

The **present perfect continuous** can be used to account for a period of time when you were expected to do something, but didn't do it. For example: *I'm sorry I didn't arrive on time, but I* ***have been running*** *late all day because my little boy is ill. I didn't go to the post office because* ***I've been ironing*** *all morning.*

C ***Complete the following sentences by adding an explanation that tells why the action wasn't done. Use the present perfect continuous tense in your sentences.***

1. I haven't walked the dog because I've been writing letters all afternoon.
2. I didn't get to see that movie because ______
3. I haven't been able to call you because ______
4. I didn't sleep last night because ______
5. We can't stop by today because ______
6. I wanted to finish the painting but ______
7. I cancelled my appointment with Dr Tan because ______
8. Jane hasn't cleaned her room yet because ______
9. My clothes are soaking wet because ______

 ISBN 978-81-8477-751-2

10. It shouldn't take me long because ______________________________

____

11. I must sit down because ______________________________

____

12. I tried to phone you but ______________________________

____

Grammar Help

The **present perfect continuous** is also used to explain why you are good at something or know something. It is often used with a **time marker**. For example: *I can speak Mandarin well because my parents have been teaching me at home* ***for five years***.

D ***Match the sentences with suitable reasons from the box to explain logically why the person in each situation is or would be good at the activity.***

- a. She's been reading every night.
- b. She's been making her own clothes for ages.
- c. He's been running around the track nightly.
- d. She has been excelling in her current work.
- e. I've been mixing paint for hours to get it.
- f. He's been driving for many years.
- g. She's been working as a chef for two years.
- h. She's been living in Spain for five years.
- i. He's been learning to play since he was six.
- j. He's been travelling for many years.

1. Lester would make a good tour guide. ______________________________

____

 ISBN 978-81-8477-751-2

2. Gina speaks perfect Spanish. ______________________________

____

3. Bob plays the piano like a professional. ______________________________

____

4. Sue is a very good reader. ______________________________

____

5. Jack is very fit. ______________________________

____

6. Jan has been given an exciting new job. ______________________________

____

____

7. Peta always appears so well dressed. ______________________________

____

8. Your mum is a great cook. ______________________________

____

9. Your dad is a very competent driver. ______________________________

____

____

10. What a great colour! ______________________________

____

 ISBN 978-81-8477-751-2

E ***What reason might be given to each comment on the left? Include a time marker in your answer in the bubble on the right.***

Karen is good at netball.

1. She has been training three times a week.

Tom always gets high marks in maths.

2. ______________________________

____

____

I wish I could draw like Sally.

3. ______________________________

____

____

Why is Harry's model so perfect?

4. ______________________________

____

____

 ISBN 978-81-8477-751-2

15 Past Perfect and Past Perfect Continuous Tenses

Grammar Help

- The **past perfect** tense is used for an action that was completed before a definite time, or before another action that took place in the past. For example: *After we* ***had finished*** *our dinner, we went to the movies.*
- The past perfect tense is formed by using **had** + **past participle**, for example: ***had washed, had eaten***.

A ***Each of the following sentences talks about two actions done in the past. Complete each sentence with a past perfect tense of the verb that talks about the earlier action. Then underline the past tense verb that talks about the action after that. The first one has been done for you.***

1. Dad called to say that he ___had forgotten___ (forget) his mobile phone.
2. They entered the house after they ________ (check) that it was safe.
3. By the time the police came, the unruly crowd ________ (disperse).
4. Dad burnt the leaves after he ________ (sweep) them into a pile.
5. The farmers stopped ploughing only after the sun ________ (set).
6. She sobbed after she ________ (hear) about my misfortune.
7. The neighbour found out who ________ (broke) his window.
8. My friend told me that he ________ (discover) a cave.
9. When we arrived, the movie ________ (start) already.
10. After she ________ (complete) her homework, she went to bed.

 ISBN 978-81-8477-751-2

Grammar Help

The **past perfect** tense is sometimes used in reported speech. For example: *Lee told me that he* ***had scored*** *two goals.*

B ***Read the following sentences and change the direct speech into reported speech. Remember to change the first or second person pronouns to the third person.***

1. "I received a letter from my pen-pal," said Bill.

   ____

2. "I didn't do it," insisted Mark.

   ____

3. "Who has borrowed my pen?" asked Jane.

   ____

4. "We've already washed the dishes," reported Bob.

   ____

5. "I've got to leave early," apologized Sam.

   ____

6. "I saw an accident on the way to school," said Tom.

   ____

7. "I've lost my mother," sobbed the little girl.

   ____

8. "I've read the book you lent me," said John to me.

   ____

9. Terry suggested, "Let me take over because I've had my lunch earlier."

   ____

 ISBN 978-81-8477-751-2

C ***Complete these newspaper sentences using the past perfect tense form of the verbs in the box and other suitable words.***

engulf	return	clear	cause	embezzle
sustain	collide	strike	reach	break into

1. Eyewitnesses reported that the two vehicles ______________________________

   ____

2. It was Thursday before relatives of the victim noticed that he ______________________________

   ____

3. The thief confessed that he ______________________________

   ____

4. Parliament resumed today after the Prime Minister ______________________________

   ____

5. Farmers reported that heavy rainfall ______________________________

   ____

6. Within an hour, the jury ______________________________

   ____

7. By the time the fire fighters arrived, the flames ______________________________

   ____

8. The extent of the damage could be seen after the smoke ______________________________

   ____

9. An oil tanker sank off the Alaskan coast after it ______________________________

   ____

10. The accountant stood in the dock and admitted that he ______________________________

    ____

 ISBN 978-81-8477-751-2

Grammar Help

- The **past perfect continuous** tense is used to talk about actions that were going on in the past when something happened. For example: ***I had been sailing** for two hours when the mast snapped.*
- The past perfect continuous tense is formed by using **had** + **been** + **present participle**. For example: ***had been washing, had been eating***

D ***Column A contains information about something Amy was doing in the past. Column B contains information about something that happened while she was doing it. Use this information to make sentences. Be sure to use the past perfect continuous tense for the actions in Column A, and the simple past tense for the actions given in Column B. The first one has been done for you.***

Column A	Column B
1. practising the violin for three hours	a string snapped and hit her in the face
2. building a sandcastle at the beach	a crab nipped her toe
3. sleeping on the sofa	her dog jumped on her and woke her up
4. shopping in the mall	a thief grabbed her bag and ran away
5. playing netball at school	it started to rain
6. climbing a ladder	a rung broke and she fell
7. visiting her mum in hospital	slipped and bruised her shin
8. enjoying dinner	swallowed a small fish bone and had to go to hospital
9. sewing for an hour	she pricked her finger with the needle and it bled
10. watching a film	she spilt her drink and popcorn all over her dress

 ISBN 978-81-8477-751-2

1. Amy had been practising for three hours when a string on her violin snapped and hit her in the face.

2.

3.

4.

5.

6.

7.

8.

9.

10.

 ISBN 978-81-8477-751-2

16 Expressing Future Time

Grammar Help

- The modals **shall** or **will** are used with the pronouns **I** and **we** when you talk about future happenings.
- Most people use **will** when they make future promises and threats.
- You generally use **I/we shall** to express the future and **I/we will** to make a promise or threat, while **he/they shall** shows obligation. For example: *They **shall** be here on time* (or else!).

A ***Predict what the speaker will say in each of the situations. Use will or shall + verb in your answers. Then decide if it is a promise, threat or simple expression of a future action. The first one has been done for you.***

1. "If you don't stop squabbling, I will turn off the television and send you to bed," warned Mother. ____________

2. "To make sure our team wins the final, we ____________ every day before the match," explained the coach. ____________

3. Nathan told his teacher, "To make sure the playground is clean and attractive, my friend and I ____________ ____________." ____________

4. "I know smoking is bad for my health, so I ____________ ____________," promised Mr Brown. ____________

5. Sean's mother told him, "Your computer is meant to help you study. It's not for playing games. If you don't use it for the right purpose, I ____________ ____________." ____________

 ISBN 978-81-8477-751-2

6. "I can't cycle this afternoon because I promised Mum I would come straight home from school. However, I ________________ tomorrow," Paul assured his friend. ____________

7. "If you are very good today, I ________________ ________________. I know you want to see that new film at the Lido," Mother said with a smile. ____________

8. "If you add hot water to ice, it ________________ ________________," predicted the little boy. ____________

9. "If they drop the price of that car next month, I ________ ________________ for you," promised her husband. ____________

10. "You ________________ if you continue to ignore the rules: I ________________ sure of that," promised the Principal. ____________

Grammar Help

You can use ***about to*** + **verb** when you talk about an action that will happen in the immediate or near future.

B ***Read the following situations and complete the last sentence using about to to describe an action that will happen in the immediate future. The first one is done for you.***

1. Ann has completed her homework and has placed it in her school bag. She has turned off the television, brushed her teeth and put on her pyjamas.

   She is about to go to bed.

2. Dr Kamal has said goodbye to his wife and children, picked up his briefcase and opened the car door.

   He ________________________________

 ISBN 978-81-8477-751-2

3. The passengers have fastened their safety belts. The attendants are seated. The plane has taxied to the runway and the engines are revving.

   They ______________________________

4. Tom is walking towards the court. He has a tennis racquet in his hand and a bottle of water and some new balls in his sports bag.

   He ______________________________

5. Mr and Mrs Green are dressed in their best clothes. Mr Green has theatre tickets. A taxi has just turned into their driveway.

   They ______________________________

6. Mr Martin has printed off the agenda, picked up his files and told his secretary to take any messages. He enters the Board Room.

   He ______________________________

7. The children have packed the sandwiches, drinks, a tent and a blanket. They have insect repellent and a camera.

   They ______________________________

8. Jane is studying every night and so are all her friends. They are all very nervous.

   They ______________________________

9. Dr Packer is scrubbing his hands. The patient is ready and the nurses are standing by with his instruments and surgical gloves.

   Dr Packer ______________________________

10. The runners are all in position. The starter raises his gun. Everyone is tense.

    The race ______________________________

 ISBN 978-81-8477-751-2

Grammar Help

You use **will / shall + be + present participle** to talk about events that have been planned or are likely to happen. This is known as the **future continuous tense.**

C ***Complete the future continuous verb in each of the following sentences to show that an event has been planned or is likely to happen. The first one is done for you.***

1. This time tomorrow, **I will be** ___flying___ to Europe with my grandmother.
2. Next Thursday, **I shall be** ______________ my birthday with my friends.
3. After school on Friday, **I will be** ______________ my friends at the shopping mall.
4. Next Saturday morning, **I will be** ______________ my grandma in hospital.
5. During the lunch break tomorrow, **I shall be** ______________ my book to the library.
6. At 8:00 pm on Friday, my favourite band **will be** ______________ at the concert hall.
7. At 8:30 am on Wednesday, we **will be** ______________ in the school hall during some boring talk.
8. On Sunday, my parents **will be** ______________ Aunt Sarah's wedding.
9. In four years' time, **I will be** ______________ secondary school.
10. When my brother is 18, he **will be** ______________ national service.
11. It's very late. When you get home, be very quiet as your family **will be** ______________.
12. Have you any idea of what you **will be** ______________ for the class picnic on Friday?

 ISBN 978-81-8477-751-2

D ***Read the clues and predict what will be taking place in each situation. Use will be + present participle in your answers. The first one has been done for you.***

1. Mr Green has made arrangements with his boss. He has placed his golf clubs in the car.

   Mr Green will be playing golf with his boss.

2. Amy has made plans to meet Samantha in the library. It is exam week.

3. Nelson's bike has a puncture and he has soccer practice this evening.

4. Miss Danker is the treasurer for the Garden Society. It meets on the first Saturday of the month. The next day is the first Saturday in June.

5. Betsy has a part-time job in a fashion store where she works on weekends only. The next day is Saturday.

6. Aunt Kathy has a broken pipe in the bathroom. She talks to a plumber on the phone.

7. Shirley is booked on a flight to London. She is studying overseas.

8. Ben has the flu and his father fixes a doctor's appointment for him.

9. The Prime Minister's secretary has notified the school. The school has been thoroughly cleaned. A red carpet has been laid down.

 ISBN 978-81-8477-751-2

10. The garage paint is peeling. Dad buys some overalls, paint brushes and some white paint.

11. Mrs Smith buys some ingredients and twelve candles at the supermarket. Mr Smith blows up a hundred balloons. Sophie Smith is very excited. Invitations have been sent.

12. Tim's friend, Patrick, is sick. Tim prepares a basket of fruit and a get-well card. He checks which bus to catch and phones to find out about visiting hours.

13. Protective hoarding is put around the Capitol Theatre. Danger signs are prominently placed in the street. The demolition team makes a final check of the equipment.

14. The prisoner completes digging a tunnel. He makes a dummy to place on his bed. The guards are not suspicious. He believes his plan is foolproof.

15. Kelly works for a popular television station. She is often asked to appear in the "Saturday Live Show" whenever a host is ill. The host of the show has a bad sore throat today.

 ISBN 978-81-8477-751-2

17 Simple and Compound Sentences

Grammar Help

- A **simple sentence** has only one clause.
- A **compound sentence** has two or more clauses that can stand on their own. The clauses in a compound sentence are equally important.

A ***Read the folowing sentences. Write an S in the box next to each simple sentence and a C next to each compound sentence.***

1. Kim likes chess. ☐
2. Please stand up and let the old lady have your seat. ☐
3. The sun is out today. ☐
4. We can go fishing. ☐
5. You can read or you can watch television. ☐
6. The children like swimming. ☐
7. Wild animals eat raw meat, but domestic animals prefer cooked meat. ☐
8. John woke up early, but Susan slept until noon. ☐
9. The fans cheered their team. ☐
10. The children tricked the witch. ☐
11. We couldn't find the house, so we went home. ☐
12. The patient seemed to be in good spirits. ☐
13. Cheetahs are very swift animals. ☐
14. They dashed to the bus-stop, but they were too late for the bus. ☐
15. They left the supermarket at nine o'clock. ☐

 ISBN 978-81-8477-751-2

Grammar Help

There are three main types of **simple sentences**.

Type 1: It has a subject, a transitive verb and an object. The subject does something directly to the object.
For example: *The cat caught the mouse.*

Type 2: It has a subject and a verb, but no object. The verb is intransitive. The subject does something, but not to an object.
For example: *The cat meowed loudly.*

Type 3: It has a subject and a verb **be**.
For example: *The boys* ***were*** *excited. Cats* ***are*** *mammals.*

B ***Underline the verb in each of the following sentences. Put a tick under the correct heading that describes the type of sentence. If the verb is transitive, circle the object of that verb. The first one has been done for you.***

	Type 1	Type 2	Type 3
1. The actors played (their parts) brilliantly.	✓	☐	☐
2. A violin is a stringed instrument.	☐	☐	☐
3. The disturbed parrots flew off.	☐	☐	☐
4. The family packed their camping gear.	☐	☐	☐
5. The team members felt very optimistic about their chances.	☐	☐	☐
6. The mountains reverberated with the echo.	☐	☐	☐
7. Dinosaurs are extinct animals.	☐	☐	☐
8. The fans enthusiastically cheered their favourite band.	☐	☐	☐
9. The baby remained asleep.	☐	☐	☐
10. The burglar forced open the door.	☐	☐	☐

 ISBN 978-81-8477-751-2

Grammar Help

You can link two clauses to form a **compound sentence** with **coordinating conjunctions: or, and, so, but, yet.** For example: *He tried very hard **but** he didn't succeed. Anne washed the dishes **and** I watered the plants.*

C ***Read the following passage and add the coordinating conjunctions* and, or, so *or* but *in the appropriate spaces to complete the compound sentences.***

"You must hurry (1) ________________ you will miss your bus," urged Mrs Adams. Ben was hurrying (2) ________________ he couldn't find his other blue sock anywhere. He looked high (3) ________________ he looked low (4) ________________ the sock seemed to have disappeared.

"You could use your new ones (5) ________________ you could wear an odd pair," suggested Mrs Adams. Ben wanted to wear his new socks to Linda's party on Saturday, (6) ________________ he didn't want to open the packet.

"I could wear my sandals (7) ________________ I could wear sports socks with trainers," thought Ben. "Yes, I'll wear my trainers (8) ________________ I'll wear my white socks." He put them on (9) ________________ rushed to the door, (10) ________________ he knew it was too late.

"You could run to school (11) ________________ I could drive you in the car," smiled Mrs Adams. Ben was very grateful. He made it to school just as the bell rang.

 ISBN 978-81-8477-751-2

D ***Make these sets of simple sentences into a compound sentence by using a suitable coordinating conjunction from the box.***

but	and	or	so

1. You can make an effort. You can continue being lazy.

   ____

2. I missed the last bus. I had to walk to the train station.

   ____

3. Vegetables today can be grown hydroponically. Vegetables today can be protected with pesticides.

   ____

   ____

4. Your father needs some help. Please help your father.

   ____

5. We dashed into the room. We saw that the thieves had already left.

   ____

6. I could have had a room with a view. I could have had an economy room.

   ____

   ____

7. I chose the cheapest room. I was happy with my choice.

   ____

8. The young ballerinas made many errors. The audience didn't laugh.

   ____

   ____

9. It was a hot day. Mother was tired. I made a drink for Mother.

   ____

10. You have finished your work. You can play football. You can watch television. You cannot do both.

    ____

    ____

 ISBN 978-81-8477-751-2

E ***Complete each of the following sentences using the given conjunction to form an appropriate clause.***

1. She couldn't go to camp, so ____.
2. We had a great time, but ____.
3. Our apartment is rather small, so ____.
4. She worked until very late, yet ____.
5. She was so tired she couldn't watch television or ____.
6. She folded her best clothes and ____.
7. Not only are you disgracefully dirty, but ____.
8. He walked to the end of the street and ____.
9. He knew he had no hope of winning the race, yet ____.
10. She has an excellent ear for music, but ____.
11. He not only washed the car, but ____.
12. We cannot go away these holidays because ____.

 ISBN 978-81-8477-751-2

18 Clauses and Complex Sentences

Grammar Help

A **complex sentence** has one **main clause** and one or more **subordinate clauses**. For example: ***I have a shower*** before I go to bed. The main clause is in bold print and the subordinate clause is underlined.

- Main clauses are **independent clauses** because they make sense on their own, apart from the rest of the sentence. Subordinate clauses depend on the main clause and do not make sense on their own. So they are also called **dependent clauses**.
- **Subordinating conjunctions** are used to link the main and subordinate clauses to form complex sentences. The subordinating conjunction used in the example above is **before.**

A ***Match each main clause in Column A with a suitable subordinate clause in Column B to form a complex sentence. Write your complete sentences on the next page.***

COLUMN A	COLUMN B
1. Jane sighed with relief	• since her mother had a headache
2. I'm going to help the new student	• in order to win the scholarship
3. He worked so hard	• as she did not understand the jokes
4. I came early	• that perspiration dripped from his brow
5. Tom's old aunt did not enjoy the show	• as much as my mother does
6. He laughed so much	• because she realized she would not have to sing solo
7. Jan thought it best to turn off the music	• as it had been raining all night
8. The sun was so hot	• so that he will have less trouble adjusting to this school
9. My sister is so lazy	• so that I could help you prepare for the party
10. My father doesn't like pears	• that she prefers to go hungry than to make a sandwich to eat
11. He studied very hard	• that tears rolled down his cheeks
12. We cancelled the picnic	• that his health was seriously affected

 ISBN 978-81-8477-751-2

1.

2.

3.

4.

5.

6.

7.

8.

9.

10.

11.

12.

 ISBN 978-81-8477-751-2

Grammar Help

If a subordinate clause gives more information about a verb in a sentence, it is known as an adverbial clause. The example, *I have a shower* ***before I go to bed,*** has an adverbial clause of time, which is shown in bold print.

- An **adverbial clause of reason** answers the question **"why?"** for the action in the main clause.
- An **adverbial clause of purpose** answers the question **"what for?"** for the action in the main clause.
- An **adverbial clause of result** tells you the result of the action in the main clause.
- An **adverbial clause of comparison** compares the action in the main clause with another thing.

B ***Underline the subordinate clause in each of the following sentences and say whether it is an adverbial clause of reason, purpose, result or comparison. The first one is done for you as an example.***

1. Mrs Carter arranged a car pool so that she didn't have to drive her daughter to school every day. purpose
2. There will be a fire drill tomorrow so that you will all be prepared for an emergency. ______
3. In order for the games to be a success, the committee began planning months ahead. ______
4. Since you don't want to be friends with me, I won't invite you to my party. ______
5. The concert was better than I expected. ______
6. We left early for the theatre so that we would be sure to get a seat. ______
7. The Principal banned us from playing tag games because he was worried about safety. ______
8. The surf was so dangerous that the beach had to be closed. ______
9. You must exercise every day in order to stay healthy. ______

 ISBN 978-81-8477-751-2

10. That fat girl eats less than I do. ____________

11. As you don't seem interested in going to the concert, I've cancelled the tickets. ____________

12. So that she could enjoy the spring weather, Jane read her book outside in the garden. ____________

13. She couldn't help laughing because Ted looked so comical when he fell. ____________

14. My brother doesn't like reading as much as I do. ____________

15. He behaved so badly that his parents swore never to take him out again. ____________

16. I won't bother you with all the details, as I'm sure they will bore you. ____________

C ***Read the following recount. Choose a suitable word from the box to complete each of the noun clauses. You will have to use some of the words more than once.***

whether	**that**	**what**	**why**

I had a terrible fright this morning when the radio broadcaster announced (1) ____________ there had been a serious accident at the train station. I didn't know (2) ____________ had happened or (3) ____________ my sister had already left for work, but I had heard her tell Mum last night (4) ____________ she wanted to catch the early train today. I wasn't sure (5) ____________ she needed to go so early or (6) ____________ she had to do that was so important. I just knew (7) ____________ my sister might have been injured. For a moment, I didn't know (8) ____________ I should do. But then I realized that the sensible thing would be to see (9) ____________ she was still in her bed. I raced into her room only to find (10) ____________ she was sound asleep.

 ISBN 978-81-8477-751-2

Grammar Help

Some sentences are joined by relative pronouns such as **who, which, that** and **whose** to form complex sentences.

D ***Choose a suitable relative pronoun from the box to combine each pair of sentences into a complex sentence.***

whose	that	who	which

1. That girl over there is my friend. She helps me when I have difficulty with my schoolwork.

____

____

2. I bought chocolates instead of a sandwich. That didn't please my mother.

____

3. This is the dog. It followed me home last night.

____

4. That lady is my teacher. Her uncle is a well-known scientist.

____

5. Jack found a wallet. It had been reported stolen.

____

6. My father's vintage car was purchased by a man. The man really appreciates artifacts of the past.

____

____

7. I chose to stay home and read a novel. I borrowed it from the library yesterday.

____

8. The clumsy waitress slipped and fell. She was carrying a tray of drinks.

____

 ISBN 978-81-8477-751-2

E ***Read the following news report. Nine of the clauses are in bold print. Write "N" over the noun clauses, "Adj" over the adjectival clauses, and "Adv" over the adverbial clauses. Can you find any more of these clauses? Underline the clauses you have found.***

It was announced today that Mark Green, **who was from Denmark Primary School,** has won first prize in the prestigious Young Writers Essay Competition. In presenting the prize, the judging panel acknowledged **that this year's standard of entries was particularly high.**

Mark's story, **which took just one day to write,** was chosen from three hundred entries. Mark's writing style, which is very mature for his age, received high praise from all five judges. "Not many twelve-year-old students can write **as well as he,**" stated the head of the panel.

Mark, **whose parents are teachers,** has not always been a good writer. At first he found writing difficult **because the other children teased him** about his poor grammar. So, in order to improve it, he did writing exercises after school. He tried **so hard that he was writing five essays a week.**

Mark seemed embarrassed by all the fuss. When asked **whether he planned to become an author,** Mark replied that he wasn't sure. With this prize to his credit, I am sure **he has a bright future ahead.**

 ISBN 978-81-8477-751-2

19 Conditional Clauses

Grammar Help

There are three main kinds of conditionals. The first of these is called the **first conditional**. It is used to show an event that is likely to happen, or to warn people.

- The conditional clause can begin with **if** or **unless**. For example: ***If** we are early, we will definitely get tickets. **Unless** we are early, we will not get tickets.*
- The first conditional clause is usually in the present tense. The main clause may be in the future tense. For example: *If you **like**, I will wait for you. I will be angry, unless you **wait** for me.*
- The main clause can be in the present tense too. For example: *If I read too much, I **become** tired. Unless I read at night, I **can't get** to sleep.*
- The main clause can also have an imperative verb. For example: *If you see Kim, **tell** her the good news. If anyone phones, **write** down their number for me.*

A ***Complete each of the following first conditionals, using the verb in brackets. Be sure to use the correct tense. An example is done for you.***

1. If you continue to be mean, I will certainly go home. ______ (go)
2. If it snows, ______ (wear)
3. You will not get good grades ______ ______ (study)
4. The cat will scratch you ______ (threaten)
5. The other team will win ______ ______ (train)
6. If you find the maths problems difficult, ______ ______ (help)
7. The plants will die ______ (water)
8. If you walk here with bare feet, ______ ______ (cut)

 ISBN 978-81-8477-751-2

Grammar Help

The **second conditional** is used when you want to talk about possible, but unlikely, situations in the future. For example: ***If you were a millionaire,*** *what would you do with your money?*

To make a second conditional sentence, you use an **if-clause** with a **past tense verb** and a main clause that contains **would** + **infinitive**. For example: *If I* ***won*** *the lottery, I* ***would buy*** *my family a new car.*

B ***Although the following situations are unlikely, what would you do if they should happen to you?***

1. You walked out of the restaurant by mistake without paying for your meal.

   If I walked out of the restaurant accidentally without paying, I would return and apologize for my mistake.

2. You lost your train ticket and you didn't have any money to get home.

   ____

   ____

3. You knew your friend had been teasing a smaller child.

   ____

   ____

4. Your parents went away for the weekend and left you in charge of your little brother or sister.

   ____

   ____

5. The lift in your apartment block stopped at the 18th floor and wouldn't move.

   ____

   ____

 ISBN 978-81-8477-751-2

6. You rode home from school on the wrong bicycle.

7. You were made Principal for a day.

8. You wrote a bestselling novel.

9. Your parents sent you to school in Spain.

10. You were given two tickets to the FA Cup finals.

11. You saved up one thousand dollars.

12. Your fairy godmother gave you one wish.

 ISBN 978-81-8477-751-2

Grammar Help

The **third conditional** is used to show impossible events that cannot be carried out because they are past events and the opportunity for accomplishing them is no longer possible.

In the third conditional, the ***if*-clause** is in the past perfect tense (***had*** + **past participle**). The main clause usually has **would** or **could** or **might** + **have** + **past participle**.

C ***What could the person/people have done in each of the following situations? Use the third conditional in your answer. The first one is done for you.***

1. If you had booked the tickets early, you would have been able to see the performance.
2. If you had arrived late, ______________________
3. If she had been more careful, ______________________
4. If the people had heeded the warning, ______________________
5. If only I had known that, ______________________
6. If he had kept his promise, ______________________
7. If you had brought the dog to the vet, ______________________
8. If you hadn't found your passport, ______________________

 ISBN 978-81-8477-751-2

D Add a suitable present or past tense verb to complete each conditional sentence.

1. If the temperature falls, people ________________ warm clothes.
2. If you place ice in the sun, it ________________ .
3. If a cat is contented, it ________________ .
4. If an elephant in a herd is in distress, the others ________________ to help it.
5. If the hounds pick up a scent, they ________________ their prey until they corner it.
6. If the poles on two magnets are opposite, they ________________ each other.
7. In the Stone Age, if people had no fire, they ________________ their meat raw.
8. If you don't have an umbrella, you ________________ wet in the rain.

E Read the following passage and add a suitable present tense verb of your own choice in each blank space.

My Little Brother

I just don't know what to do with my stubborn little brother. He always does the opposite to what I want him to do. If I ask him to run, he (1) ________________ . If I want him to stand up, he (2) ________________ and if I suggest that he whispers, he (3) ________________ . Sometimes I take pictures of him, and if I ask him to smile, he (4) ________________ . He is very frustrating. If I cry when I fall off my bike, he (5) ________________ and if I have fun with my friends, he (6) ________________ me.

Do you have a sibling like this? However, despite his annoying habits I still love him.

 ISBN 978-81-8477-751-2

Revision Test

Section 1 (25 marks)

A ***Choose the best answer for each blank and write its number in the brackets provided. (15 marks)***

1. Everyone except Amy ____________ coming to my birthday party today.

   (1) is　　(2) are

   (3) was　　(4) were　　( )

2. Mark was disappointed to hear that most of the boys ____________ the early train because they had slept in.

   (1) miss　　(2) were missing

   (3) would miss　　(4) had missed　　( )

3. Mum told me to divide the ice cream ____________ my five friends.

   (1) among　　(2) with

   (3) between　　(4) over　　( )

4. Tom is my English friend ____________ is visiting Singapore next week.

   (1) whom　　(2) which

   (3) who　　(4) whose　　( )

5. Although we were cold and hungry, we told ____________ not to despair.

   (1) ourself　　(2) themselves

   (3) us　　(4) ourselves　　( )

6. Can you tell me ____________ he looks like?

   (1) how　　(2) which

   (3) what　　(4) that　　( )

7. ____________ you help me with the cleaning, you will not get any pocket money to spend.

   (1) If　　(2) Unless

   (3) Since　　(4) Because　　( )

 ISBN 978-81-8477-751-2

8. There are only ____________ more days left before the holidays start.

(1) a little (2) many

(3) much (4) a few ( )

9. I ____________ this way many times before and I still get lost.

(1) am travelling (2) travelled

(3) have travelled (4) had travelled ( )

10. I prefer skate-boarding ____________ playing computer games.

(1) with (2) to

(3) than (4) for ( )

11. The lifeguard was swimming ____________ the tide.

(1) along (2) above

(3) to (4) against ( )

12. All the children ____________ to pass the exam so they are studying very hard.

(1) tried (2) were trying

(3) are trying (4) is trying ( )

13. If I come, you will let me play too, ____________ you?

(1) will (2) would

(3) won't (4) wouldn't ( )

14. Please show me ____________ to get to the post office from here.

(1) when (2) where

(3) what (4) how ( )

15. That book has my name in it, so it must be ____________ .

(1) ours (2) theirs

(3) mine (4) my ( )

 ISBN 978-81-8477-751-2

B ***Read each sentence carefully and underline the correct word or words in the brackets. (10 marks)***

16. When I heard the bells ______________ (rung, rang, ring), I knew I was late.

17. You ______________ (could, should, might) tell what really happened so we know the truth.

18. "I ______________ (will cook, am cooking, cooked) dinner as soon as I return from the market," promised Mother.

19. The strikers refused to go back to work ______________ (since, for, until) their demands are met.

20. Nobody wants Bob on their team because he ______________ (frequently, seldom, occasionally) obeys the rules.

21. Dad warned us not to place our things ______________ (along, beside, against) the wall he had just painted.

22. The children ______________ (are sleeping, were sleeping, was sleeping) when their father returned from work.

23. Neither that boy nor the girl with him ______________ (are, were, is) from our school.

24. John plays for the team ______________ (which, who, whom) wins every season.

25. Mrs Green had tidied the house just before her friend ______________ (turned down, turned up, turned over).

 ISBN 978-81-8477-751-2

Section 2: Cloze Passages (25 marks)

C ***Fill in each blank with the most appropriate word from the box. There will be three words left over when you have completed the exercise.* (15 marks)**

among	there	into	when	why	after
many	their	for	an	few	little
whose	could	at	to	and	before

The teachers (26) ____________ the Principal of our local neighbourhood school are planning (27) ____________ set up (28) ____________ activity club on the school premises.

The club will be for students (29) ____________ both parents go to work. It is aimed (30) ____________ providing after-school care, allowing students to complete their homework and encouraging cooperation (31) ____________ them.

In every class in the school, there are (32) ____________ students who return home to an empty apartment or house (33) ____________ the school day finishes, and this is (34) ____________ they are most likely to get (35) ____________ trouble. With (36) ____________ to keep them occupied and no adult supervision, it is not surprising that some of them get into mischief. Some children are unsupervised for up to six hours (37) ____________ an adult comes home. Others are expected to clean and cook for (38) ____________ parents. Very (39) ____________ of these students complete their homework every night.

An activity club (40) ____________ address these problems and set students back onto an academic pathway to success—I think this is an excellent idea.

 ISBN 978-81-8477-751-2

D ***Fill in each blank with the most appropriate word from the box. There will be five words left over when you have completed the exercise. (10 marks)***

across	**everybody**	**his**	**on**	**onto**
whose	**someone**	**my**	**over**	**in**
their	**nobody**	**our**	**who**	**as**

Martha is talking to a television reporter (41) ____________ is covering a local news story. Here is Martha's account of the incident.

"I looked around when I heard the scream and to (42) ____________ horror I saw an enormous bunch of balloons floating (43) ____________ the sky. Hanging (44) ____________ tightly was a small boy who looked about three years old. (45) ____________ mother was screaming frantically for (46) ____________ to help her, but (47) ____________ knew what to do. The situation looked hopeless until a police officer walking on the opposite footpath ran (48) ____________ the road and jumped (49) ____________ a car roof. He grabbed hold of the boy's legs and caught him just in time, (50) ____________ the boy's numbed fingers lost their hold on the balloons. There is no doubt that the police officer saved the boy's life."

Section 1:	**/25**
Section 2:	**/25**
TOTAL	**/50**

 ISBN 978-81-8477-751-2

Page 1

A 2. I'm an acrobat.
3. I'm a caddie.
4. I'm a chauffer.
5. I'm an architect.
6. I'm a milliner.
7. I'm an heiress.
8. I'm an auctioneer.
9. I'm a judge.
10. I'm an ornithologist.
11. I'm a herald.

Page 2

B 1. a 2. the 3. the
4. the 5. a 6. the
7. a 8. the 9. the
10. the 11. a 12. an
13. an 14. the 15. A

C 1. the 2. — 3. —
4. — 5. a 6. —
7. — 8. an 9. the
10. — 11. the 12. the
13. the 14. the 15. the
16. the 17. — 18. the
19. a 20. the 21. —
22. the 23. the 24. a
25. the 26. an 27. a
28. — 29. the 30. the
31. the 32. a 33. the
34. the

Page 4

D 2. the sick 3. the aged
4. the educated 5. the poor
6. the rich 7. the generous
8. the adventurous

Page 5

A 1. a few 2. some, much
3. some 4. a little
5. much 6. more
7. any 8. all
9. many 10. several, plenty

Page 6

B 1. a 2. c 3. a
4. a 5. b 6. d
7. a 8. d 9. b
10. d

Page 7

C 1. neither 2. either
3. another 4. both
5. Either 6. Neither
7. either 8. another
9. both 10. another

Page 8

D L1: (circled) every, Each; (underlined) is-S
L2: (circled) both; (underlined) brings-S, are-P
L3: (circled) another, few
L4: (circled) every; (underlined) are-P
L5: (circled) both; (underlined) has-S
L6: (circled) all; (underlined) say-P, are-P
L7: (circled) all; (underlined) is-S

Page 9

E 1. a cake of 2. a pane of
3. some 4. a little
5. a slice of 6. no
7. a few drops of 8. a cup of
9. a few grains of 10. much
11. a piece of 12. a packet of
13. a bag of 14. a block of

Page 10

A *Abstract nouns*: courage, enthusiasm, will, poverty, happiness, guidance, education, knowledge, wealth, discipline, dedication, qualities, life

Page 11

B 1. freedom
2. kindness, generosity
3. loneliness
4. theft 5. childhood
6. prudence 7. insolence
8. leniency 9. laziness
10. honesty 11. envy
12. beauty 13. Pride
14. Curiosity 15. Ignorance

Page 12

C

C	R	E	A	M	B	I	T	I	O	N	T	H
A	P	E	A	C	E	B	W	I	S	E	W	O
R	E	A	C	H	A	R	I	T	Y	B	A	N
E	L	B	A	J	U	S	T	I	C	E	R	E
F	O	R	G	E	T	F	U	L	N	E	S	S
R	P	A	S	T	Y	E	N	T	A	S	K	T
E	E	V	F	A	T	A	I	J	R	K	T	Y
E	N	E	R	G	Y	R	T	U	G	I	T	O
D	A	R	C	O	W	A	Y	D	U	L	R	W
O	B	Y	C	O	U	R	A	G	E	L	U	E
M	O	D	E	S	T	Y	L	E	N	G	T	H
S	K	N	O	W	L	E	D	G	E	U	H	E

2. *Answers may vary.*

Page 13

D 1. Jack, Richard and John's brother, is visiting us tomorrow.
2. Many residents' houses were destroyed by the strong tornado winds.
3. Sarah's father's car was stolen last Friday.
4. The rose plant's thorns make the flowers difficult to pick.
5. The princesses' maids were competitive and always suspicious of the intentions of one another.
6. Peter's and Mary's mothers wept at their wedding.
7. The hermit crab's habit of changing its shell as it grows puts it in danger.
8. The volcano erupted and spewed its lava on the town, burning many people's homes and destroying the town's main buildings as well.
9. Jane cleans her own bedroom, but her mother cleans her brothers' bedrooms.
10. The board of directors' spokesman gave a short statement to the press.
11. The thieves' hideout was raided by the police after they received a tipoff.
12. The mother cats' instinct is to protect their kittens from harm.

Page 15

A 1. I cannot remember my new phone number.
2. Exercising in hot weather is foolish.
3. The latest computer is very fast and easy to use.
4. I have written down the name of the book.
5. The time of the television programme was 8:00 pm.
6. Have you heard about John's good fortune?
7. The photo of my aunt on holidays was very clear.
8. The detective placed the time of the murder at about 3:00 am.

B *Answers may vary.*

Page 16

C *Noun phrases*:
something of beauty
the bridges that span the River Seine
the waters of the Seine
some of its most famous landmarks
the skyline at Champs de Mars
a huge glass prism in its courtyard
my most favourite place in the whole of Paris

Phrases in apposition:
the capital city of France
one of the most attractive of the French buildings
the river island of Île de la Cité
another monument of great appeal
once a royal palace
Leonardo da Vinci's most famous painting
the Sacre Coeur

Page 17

D 1. what was on the other side
2. nobody had been there before
3. the danger that lurked over the top of the ridge
4. rain had caused a mud slide
5. they would fall to the valley below
6. what had happened to them
7. they would be buried in mud
8. the edge of the ridge was slippery

Page 18

E 1. the one you hear barking every night
2. the one who scores the most goals
3. that the thief was guilty
4. that you helped the old lady cross the street
5. that the Earth is round
6. the boy wearing the green T-shirt
7. the one visiting him from Africa
8. that a tomato is a vegetable
9. that man walked the Earth thousands of years ago
10. the teacher who is most popular with all students
11. the one you skidded at yesterday
12. the very old man who lives near me

Page 19

F Have you heard what happened to the Man in the Moon? C
He tried to bully the dish and the spoon. P
The cow told him crossly it was not very nice; C
To continue would mean he must pay the price. C
The punishment for not saying "Please" P
Is to change forever into smelly green cheese.
But the moon just continued his bullying ways P
And was turned into cheese for the rest of his days.

Page 20

A *Nouns* (circled):
computer, computer shop, bank, sales assistant, computers, model, laptop, counter, keyboard, wait, boys, school
Adjectival phrases (underlined):

 ISBN 978-81-8477-751-2

old and outdated, next to the bank, efficient and friendly, obsolete and outmoded, up-to-date and user-friendly, on the counter, easy-to-use, three-week, in my school

Page 21

B
2. Insects are animals with six legs.
3. Arachnids are animals with eight legs.
4. Marsupials are animals with pouches.
5. Invertebrates are animals with no/ without backbones.

C *Answers may vary.*

Page 22

D
1. A geologist is a person who studies rocks.
2. A stevedore is a person who loads and unloads ships.
3. A martyr is a person who dies for a cause he/she believes in.
4. An optimist is a person who looks on the bright side of things.
5. An abattoir is a place where animals are slaughtered for sale.
6. A monastery is a place where monks live together.
7. A silo is a place where grains are stored.
8. An apiary is a place where people keep bees for honey.

E *Answers may vary.*
The adjectival clauses are:
1. where I lost my purse
2. that Sue recommended
3. for whom the coach has the most respect
4. why people cannot breathe in water
5. when plants begin to grow
6. where my parents studied
7. whose story won the prize
8. which had followed Anne home from school
9. who is wearing a white hat
10. where I was born in

Page 23

F *Answers may vary.*
The following sentences cannot be shortened:
1. This is the theatre I lost my purse <u>at</u>.
6. Over there is the school my parents studied <u>at</u>.
7. (non-defining clause)
8. (non-defining clause)

Page 24

A *Time adverbials*:
on our birthdays
on the first day
about three o'clock in the afternoon
at night
on the following day
tomorrow morning
in a week's time
at Christmas time last year
last December
on Saturday
two weeks from today

Page 25

B
1. early, early 2. tomorrow, today
3. before 4. soon
5. once, twice 6. before
7. late, never 8. while

C
1. every evening
2. From time to time
3. instantly
4. last week
5. hardly ever
6. since that Monday
7. From time to time
8. Every day
9. in the evenings
10. For a whole week now

NOTE: 6 and 10 are interchangeable

Page 27

D
1. here, outdoors
2. overnight, still, late, tomorrow
3. dramatically, defensively
4. often, rarely, seldom, never, sometimes, yearly
5. permanently, temporarily

Page 28

E *Answers may vary.*

Page 29

A
1. much 2. hardly
3. almost / nearly 4. partially
5. quite 6. nearly / almost
7. partly 8. rather

Page 30

B *These headlines have adverbs of degree (underlined):*
1. Man <u>almost</u> killed by tiger
2. Farmhouse <u>totally</u> destroyed by fire
4. Weather <u>rather</u> warm for winter says Met Service
5. Manager admits football fans behaved <u>very</u> badly
7. Young mother <u>seriously</u> injured in car crash
8. Trade figures <u>slightly</u> lower than last year
9. Police <u>completely</u> outnumbered in riot
13. Palace officials say Princess is "<u>much</u> better"

Page 31

C
2. particularly boring
3. just about read
4. far prefer
5. nearly finished
6. pretty wealthy
7. quite poor
8. very contented
9. almost drowned
10. exceptionally fast
11. extremely brave
12. unusually thin
13. fairly heavy
14. totally submerged
15. really lucky

Page 32

D *Suggested answers*
1. John will have "nearly finished all his homework by Saturday". Also he has "just about read all the books in the school library".
2. He is "very contented to go without computer games as long as he can visit the library every day".
3. On weekends, the writer far prefers to laze around, instead of attending to his books.
4. John cannot buy computer games because his family is quite poor.
5. The writer says John is a hero because he saved the writer when he almost drowned.
6. John is much thinner than the writer, who says he is quite heavy.
7. The writer is quite heavy, and the river is flowing exceptionally fast.
8. The writer says he is "really lucky to have such a fantastic friend".

Page 33

E
1. He was <u>deeply</u> hurt because she had <u>completely</u> forgotten to call him back, despite the fact that she had promised to do so on several occasions. However, he felt <u>much</u> better when she called to apologise the next day.
2. It was the worst game the team had ever played and they had been <u>soundly</u> beaten. The players in the changing room were looking <u>absolutely</u> depressed. However the coach seemed <u>fairly</u> optimistic that the team would do better next time.
3. Mary thought that it was <u>entirely</u> Jane's own fault. She had <u>hardly</u> studied for the exam despite several reminders from the teacher and her parents. Now she had <u>almost</u> failed an exam that should have been easy for <u>such</u> a talented student.
4. The children have been cooperating <u>rather</u> well these holidays. Jack has <u>almost</u> completed his school project and Jane has <u>partially</u> completed hers. But, Betsy is the star. She has <u>completely</u> finished.
5. I had <u>hardly</u> finished eating my evening meal, when I heard a <u>quite</u> loud rapping on my front door. Upon opening it, I could <u>scarcely</u> believe my eyes.
6. It was a <u>fairly</u> small creature with <u>incredibly</u> blue eyes. Meg had found it down by the <u>nearly</u> empty water tank. It must have been <u>terribly</u> thirsty because it was frantically licking the tiny drips that seeped from the mouth of the leaking tap.

Page 34

A *Adjectives* (circled): living (2X), surprising, land-living, flying, digging

Gerunds (underlined): studying, swimming, escaping, moving, classifying (2X)

Page 35

B
1. cycling 2. Surfing
3. painting 4. baking
5. cheating 6. Hiking
7. Skipping 8. Racing
9. making 10. stealing
11. paying 12. relying
13. working 14. ageing
15. sweltering

Page 36

C
1. window-shopping
2. letter writing
3. rock climbing
4. baby sitting
5. paper toling
6. tap dancing
7. water skiing
8. marathon running

 ISBN 978-81-8477-751-2

Page 37

D 2. rod and reel
3. roller blades
4. easel
5. board and sail
6. binoculars
7. music stand
8. sewing kit
9. helmet, pump
10. stopwatch

Page 38

E *Suggested answers*
2. It is easier speaking Mandarin than reading it.
3. Sparing the rod means spoiling the child.
4. Seeing is believing.
5. Running is faster than jogging.
6. Giving is better than receiving.
7. Erring is human but forgiving is divine.
8. Helping others often means giving up your own priorities.
9. Being a good citizen means putting society's needs before your own.
10. Parking in the city is more difficult than finding a parking space in a suburban shopping centre.

Page 39

A 1. fallen through, fallen on, fell back, fallen behind, fall back on, fallen out, fallen off, fall in, fall out, falling in with
2. (a) fall in (b) fallen through
(c) fallen off (d) falling in with
(e) fallen on (f) fallen out

Page 40

B 1. disapproves of 2. depends on
3. blew up 4. put away
5. ran out of 6. burnt down
7. calls for 8. moved out of
9. turn down 10. carried out

Page 41

C 1. c 2. e 3. d
4. f 5. g 6. h
7. a 8. b

Page 42

D 1. break down (e)
break out (d)
break through (b)
break into (c)
break off (a)
2. (a) broke into
(b) break down
(c) break off
(d) break out
(e) break through

Page 43

A *All underlined verbs to be changed to past forms. It is possible to use* ***used to*** *and* ***would*** *interchangeably here.*
1. Every day, they would arise early to fetch ...
2. Then they would prepare food ...
3. ... during which the women used to put on ....
4. ... so the women would serve the food they had cooked ...
5. Some women would spend the afternoon ...
6. ... all of them used to bathe before ....
7. ... which relations used to join the family for.
8. Friends would arrive later ....
9. Rich families used to entertain lavishly.
10. They would hire professional entertainers ...

Page 44

B *Answers may vary.*

Page 45

C *Answers may vary.*

Page 47

D *Possible answers*
2. You need to look both ways before crossing the road.
3. You need to get in queue and wait for your turn.
4. You need to wait outside until you are called for.
5. You need to ask me for permission.
6. You need to apologize and be more polite next time.
7. You need to take care of them and help them.

Page 48

A 1. raced 2. crashed
3. skittered 4. eddied
5. swooped 6. dived
7. hesitated 8. watched
9. sucked 10. swirled
11. waded 12. arose
13. beamed

Page 49

B 1. swaggered 2. lurked
3. rampaged 4. languished
5. defied 6. dramatized
7. ransacked 8. persevered

C 1. ensure, insure
2. bought, brought
3. emigrate, immigrate
4. devise
5. pedalled, peddled
6. clothe

Page 50

D 1. pleaded 2. smirked
3. sneered 4. protested
5. wailed 6. challenged
7. agreed 8. assured
9. scolded 10. apologized

Page 51

E 1. dislike / hate 2. adore
3. understand 4. wonder
5. enjoy 6. think
7. please 8. realize
9. hate / dislike 10. need

F *Answers may vary.*

Page 53

A 1. performed 2. saved
3. ran 4. tripped
5. fell 6. tried
7. saw 8. leaped / leapt
9. held 10. pulled
11. suffered 12. treated
13. took 14. praised
15. sent

Page 55

B *Possible answers (adverbials have been omitted)*
2. Mr Potts stopped at the newsagent.
3. Mr Potts carried a newspaper under his arm.
4. Mr Potts bought sweets and kept them in a shopping bag.
5. Mr Potts gave sweets to children who showed sportsmanship.
6. Mr Potts sat on the bench and talked to the children.
7. Mr Potts looked in letterbox before he entered his garden.
8. Mr Potts called out to his cat.
9. Mr Potts let the writer feed the cat for him.
10. The writer carried Mr Potts' bag home for him.
11. The writer loved stroking Mr Potts' cat's fur.
12. The writer filled the cat's dish with warm milk.

Page 57

C 2. I wish I had lots of money.
3. I wish I lived in the U.S.A.
4. I wish I owned a new Playstation.
5. I wish I had lots of friends.
6. I wish I didn't have to study.

Page 58

D 1. was standing, jostled
2. was squeezing, opened
3. fell, were closing
4. was struggling, started
5. was running, began
6. was climbing, slipped, broke
7. took, was skidding
8. coped, was shivering
9. was running, bumped

Page 60

A has lived, has suffered, has studied, has planted, have had

Page 61

B 2. have had 3. has shown
4. have chosen 5. have ... started
6. have been
7. have ... wanted
8. have convinced

Page 62

C *Possible answers*
2. The family has just finished dinner.
3. I have not picked up/ put away my books yet.
4. May has recently been/visited/gone to the dentist.
5. The new neighbours have already moved in.
6. Mr Smith has always stayed at home / lived in the country.
7. He still has not tidied up his room.
8. We have already completed our homework.
9. There has been a (flood / disaster) recently.
10. Patrick still has not learnt how to cycle.

Page 64

D *Possible answers*
1. Have you sung in a musical before?
2. Have you ever gone for / had singing lessons?
3. Has the director already heard you sing (for the part)? /Have you already had/ attended an audition?
4. Have you visited/ flown/ been to London recently?

 ISBN 978-81-8477-751-2

5. Have you read / got the playscript yet?
6. Has anyone told you what the musical is about?
7. How long has it been since you left school?
8. Have you ever wished to go on with/further your studies?
9. How much money have you earned this year?
10. Have you always wanted to sing / be a singer?

Page 66

A *Present prefect continuous:*
(ha)ve been putting, haven't been eating, (ha)ve been feeling, have ... been suffering, have been experiencing, (ha)ve been getting, have ... been taking, have ... been trying, (ha)ve been exercising, (ha)ve been working, have been teaching, have been working, (have been) ignoring, have been sitting, haven't been swimming, (ha)ve been teaching, have not been taking, have not been exercising

Page 67

B 2. He has been taking the dogs for a walk.
3. I have been helping her with a project.
4. She has been going for piano lessons.
5. I have been waiting for four hours.
6. He has been painting since high school.
7. We have been digging in the garden.
8. I have been studying for my exams and I am tired.
9. He has been visiting his uncle.
10. It has been climbing up the stairs.
11. Someone has been baking cakes.
12. She has been touring France with her Grandma.

Page 69

C *Answers may vary.*

Page 70

D
1. (j) 2. (h) 3. (i)
4. (a) 5. (c) 6. (d)
7. (b) 8. (g) 9. (f)
10. (e)

Page 72

E *Possible answers*
2. He has been doing assessment exercises every day.
3. She has been drawing since she was four.
4. He has been working on it for hours.

Page 73

A 2. entered, had checked
3. came, had dispersed
4. burnt, had swept
5. stopped, had set
6. sobbed, had heard
7. found out, had broken
8. told, had discovered
9. arrived, had started
10. had completed, went

Page 74

B 1. Bill said that he had received a letter from his pen-pal.
2. Mark insisted that he had not done it.
3. Jane asked who had borrowed her pen.
4. Bob reported that they had already washed the dishes.
5. Sam apologized that he had to leave early.
6. Tom said that he had seen an accident on the way to school.
7. The little girl sobbed that she had lost her mother.
8. John said to me that he had read the book I had lent him.
9. Terry suggested that he would take over because he had had his lunch earlier.

Page 75

C *Possible answers*
1. had collided (at high speed).
2. had sustained (minor injuries).
3. had broken into (the bank vault).
4. had returned (from an overseas trip).
5. had caused (damage to their crops).
6. had reached (a consensus).
7. had engulfed (the building completely).
8. had cleared away.
9. had struck (a submerged rock).
10. had embezzled (millions of dollars).

Page 76

D 2. Amy had been building a sandcastle at the beach, when a crab nipped her toe.
3. Amy had been sleeping on the sofa, when her dog jumped on her and woke her up.
4. Amy had been shopping in the mall, when a thief grabbed her bag and ran away.
5. Amy had been playing netball at school, when it started to rain.
6. Amy had been climbing a ladder, when a rung broke and she fell.
7. Amy had been visiting her mum in hospital, when she slipped and bruised her shin.
8. Amy had been enjoying dinner, when she swallowed a small fish bone and had to go to hospital.
9. Amy had been sewing for an hour, when she pricked her finger with the needle and it bled.
10. Amy had been watching a film, when she spilt her drink and popcorn all over her dress.

Page 78

A 2. shall train, Simple future
3. will stay back to pick up all the litter. Promise
4. will cut down and try to stop smoking. Promise
5. will take it away from you. Threat
6. shall be there, Simple future
7. will give you a treat. Promise
8. will melt the ice, Simple future
9. will buy it, Promise
10. will be sorry/ punished, will make, Threat

Page 79

B 2. is about to go to work.
3. are about to take off.
4. is about to play (a game of) tennis.
5. are about to go to the theatre.
6. is about to hold a meeting.
7. are about to go camping / on a picnic.
8. are about to take their exams.
9. is about to carry out an operation.
10. is about to begin.

Page 81

C
2. celebrating 3. meeting
4. visiting 5. returning
6. performing 7. sitting/dozing
8. attending 9. finishing
10. doing 11. sleeping
12. bringing/making

Page 82

C *Possible answers*
2. Amy will be studying in the library with Samantha.
3. Nelson will be taking the bus to soccer practice this evening.
4. Miss Danker will be going for the Garden Society meeting. They will be meeting tomorrow.
5. Betsy will be working tomorrow.
6. A plumber will be coming to fix Aunt Kathy's broken pipe.
7. Shirley will be returning to London for her studies.
8. Ben will be seeing the doctor soon.
9. The Prime Minister will be visiting the school.
10. Dad will be painting the garage.
11. Sophie will be having a birthday party. Her mother will be baking a cake.
12. Tim will be going to the hospital to visit his friend, Patrick.
13. They will be demolishing the Capitol Theatre.
14. The prisoner will be escaping from the prison.
15. Kelly will be hosting today's "Saturday Live Show".

Page 84

A
1. S 2. C 3. S
4. S 5. C 6. S
7. C 8. C 9. S
10. S 11. C 12. S
13. S 14. C 15. S

Page 85

B
2. Type 3 3. Type 2
4. Type 1 5. Type 2
6. Type 2 7. Type 3
8. Type 1 9. Type 2
10. Type 1

Page 86

C
1. or 2. but
3. and 4. but
5. or 6. so
7. or 8. and
9. and 10. but
11. or

Page 87

D 1. You can make an effort or you can continue being lazy.
2. I missed the last bus, so I had to walk to the train station.
3. Vegetables today can be grown hydroponically and protected with pesticides.
4. Your father needs some help, so please help him.

 ISBN 978-81-8477-751-2

5. We dashed in to the room but we saw that the thieves had already left.
6. I could have had a room with a view or an economy room.
7. I chose the cheapest room and I was happy with my choice.
8. The young ballerinas made many errors, but the audience didn't laugh.
9. It was a hot day and Mother was tired, so I made a drink for her.
10. You have finished your work, so you can play football or watch television, but you cannot do both.

Page 88

E *Answers may vary.*

Page 89

A
1. because she realized she would not have to sing solo
2. so that he will have less trouble adjusting to this school
3. that his health was seriously affected
4. so that I could help you prepare for the party
5. as she did not understand the jokes
6. that tears rolled down his cheeks
7. since her mother had a headache
8. that perspiration dripped from his brow
9. that she prefers to go hungry than to make a sandwich to eat
10. as much as my mother does
11. in order to win the scholarship
12. as it had been raining all night

Page 91

B
2. Purpose (so that you will ...)
3. Purpose (In order for the games ...)
4. Reason (Since you don't want ...)
5. Comparison (better than I expected)
6. Purpose (so that we would ...)
7. Reason (because he was worried ...)
8. Result (the beach had to be closed)
9. Purpose (in order to stay healthy)
10. Comparison (less than I do)
11. Reason (As you don't seem ...)
12. Purpose (So that she could ...)
13. Reason (because Ted looked so ...)
14. Comparison (as much as I do)
15. Result (his parents swore never ...)
16. Reason (as I'm sure they will bore you.)

Page 92

C
1. that 2. what
3. whether 4. that
5. why 6. what
7. that 8. what
9. whether 10. that

Page 92

D *Suggested answers*
1. That girl over there is my friend who helps me when I have difficulty with my schoolwork.
2. I bought chocolates instead of a sandwich, which didn't please my mother.
3. This is the dog that/which followed me home last night.
4. That lady, whose uncle is a well-known scientist, is my teacher.
5. Jack found a wallet that/which had been reported stolen.
6. My father's vintage car was purchased by a man who really appreciates artifacts of the past.
7. I chose to stay home and read a novel that/which I had borrowed from the library yesterday.
8. The clumsy waitress who slipped and fell was carrying a tray of drinks.

Page 94

E who was from Denmark Primary School (Adj)
that this year's standard of entries ... (N)
which took just one day to write (Adj)
as well as he (Adv)
whose parents are teachers (Adj)
because the other children teased him (Adv)
so hard that he was writing five essays a week (Adv)
whether he planned to become an author (N)
he has a bright future ahead (N)

Other clauses:
which is very mature for his age (Adj),
that he wasn't sure (N), Mark Green ... has won first prize in the ...(N)

Page 95

A *Possible answers*
2. I will wear a coat.
3. if you don't study hard. / unless you study hard.
4. if you threaten it.
5. if we don't train regularly. / unless we train regularly.
6. I will help you.
7. if you don't water them. / unless you water them.
8. you will cut your soles.

Page 96

B *Answers may vary.*

Page 98

C *Answers may vary.*

Page 99

D *Suggested answers*
1. wear / put on 2. melts
3. purrs 4. come
5. track / chase 6. attract
7. ate 8. get

E
1. walks/ crawls
2. sits down
3. shouts
4. frowns / grimaces
5. laughs / chortles
6. annoys / disturbs

Pages 100 – 104: Revision Test

A
1. (1) 2. (4)
3. (1) 4. (3)
5. (4) 6. (3)
7. (2) 8. (4)
9. (3) 10. (2)
11. (4) 12. (3)
13. (3) 14. (4)
15. (3)

B
16. ring 17. should
18. will cook 19. until
20. seldom 21. against
22. were sleeping 23. is
24. which 25. turned up

C
26. and 27. to
28. an 29. whose
30. at 31. among
32. many 33. after
34. why 35. into
36. little 37. before
38. their 39. few
40. could

D
41. who 42. my
43. in 44. on
45. His 46. someone
47. nobody 48. across
49. onto 50. as

 ISBN 978-81-8477-751-2